Texts and Monographs in Computer Science

Thomas W. Reps
Tim Teitelbaum

The Synthesizer Generator Reference Manual
Third Edition

With 79 Illustrations

Springer-Verlag New York Berlin Heidelberg
London Paris Tokyo

Thomas W. Reps
Computer Sciences Department
University of Wisconsin, Madison
1210 W. Dayton St.
Madison, WI 53706
U.S.A.

Tim Teitelbaum
Department of Computer Science
Cornell University
Upson Hall
Ithaca, NY 14853
U.S.A.

Series Editor

David Gries
Department of Computer Science
Cornell University
Upson Hall
Ithaca, NY 14853
U.S.A.

Library of Congress Cataloging-in-Publication Data
Reps, Thomas W. (Thomas William)
   The synthesizer generator reference manual.
   (Texts and monographs in computer science)
   Bibliography: p.
   Includes index.
   1. Generators (Computer programs)   2. Linking loaders
(Computer programs)   3. Computer software—Development.
I. Teitelbaum, Tim.   II. Title.   III. Series.
QA76.76.G46R46   1988 b   005.1   88-24808

Printed on acid free paper.

Camera-ready copy produced by Impressions, Inc., Madison, Wisconsin.
Printed and bound by Quinn-Woodbine, Inc., Woodbine, New Jersey.
Printed in the United States of America.

9 8 7 6 5 4 3 2 1

ISBN 0-387-96910-1 Springer-Verlag New York Berlin Heidelberg London Paris Tokyo
ISBN 3-540-96910-1 Springer-Verlag Berlin Heidelberg New York London Paris Tokyo

Preface

The Synthesizer Generator is a system for automating the implementation of language-based editing environments. The editor designer prepares a specification that includes rules defining a language's context-free abstract syntax, context-sensitive relationships, display format, and concrete input syntax. From this specification, the Synthesizer Generator creates a display editor for manipulating objects according to these rules [Reps84].

This volume, *The Synthesizer Generator Reference Manual*, is intended as the defining document of the system. A companion volume, *The Synthesizer Generator: A System for Constructing Language-Based Editors* [Reps88], provides a more tutorial description of the system; it contains numerous examples that illustrate the specification and use of generated editors, as well as chapters that explain important algorithms of the implementation.

The Synthesizer Generator is a generalization of our earlier system, the Cornell Program Synthesizer [Teitelbaum81], which was a programming environment for a specific small dialect of PL/I. It featured a display-oriented, syntax-directed editor, an incremental compiler, an execution supervisor supporting source-level debugging, and a file system containing syntactically typed program fragments.

Whereas PL/I was built into the Cornell Program Synthesizer, the Synthesizer Generator accepts a formal language definition as input. Although originally conceived as a tool for creating Synthesizer-like environments for arbitrary programming languages, the Synthesizer Generator is more broadly useful. Any textual language with a hierarchical phrase structure grammar is a candidate.

Interactive theorem proving for formal mathematics and logic, for example, has emerged as a particularly suitable application.

The design of the Synthesizer Generator reflects our unhappiness with the implementation strategy of the Cornell Program Synthesizer. Rather than the Cornell Program Synthesizer's imperative approach, the Synthesizer Generator employs a declarative approach to specifying context-sensitive analysis [Demers81]. Rules for deriving facts from the syntactic structure of objects are specified in equation schemes. Environments generated from such declarative specifications using the formalism known as an attribute grammar are, in effect, spreadsheets for structured data. Just as spreadsheets maintain arithmetic results when the definition of any cell is altered, systems produced by the Synthesizer Generator maintain the consistency of an inferred database of facts about objects as they are interactively manipulated.

Much of our research has focused on the problem of efficiently re-solving attribute equations after each editing operation. The 1982 Ph.D. Thesis of Reps addressed this problem and included a prototype system for the purpose of demonstrating the feasibility of the attribute-grammar approach to building language-based editors [Reps84a]. The present system evolved from this initial prototype.

Prior to Release 2.0, the Synthesizer Generator was largely our own work; in contrast, releases since 2.0 represent the combined effort of more than a dozen people. Very considerable contributions have been made by:

T. Burr	J. Field	D. George	M. Fingerhut
S. Ghemawat	R. Hoover	C. Lagoze	C. Marceau
S. Peckham	W. Pugh	J. Reppy	S. Sinofsky
A. Zaring			

Countless discussions with our user community have guided us in refining the design and implementation of the system. The assistance of this group is appreciatively acknowledged. The Synthesizer Generator is distributed with many of the demonstration editors that these users have prepared:

S. Ahmad	B. Alpern	R. Ashcroft	T. Ball
C. Beekhuis	M. Belmonte	T. Griffin	S. Horwitz
S. Liu	K. Mughal	A. Palchoudhuri	P. Schoaff
G. Snelting	B. Vander Zanden		

As always, discussions with Alan Demers have been invaluable. We are indebted to David Gries for his careful reading of the manuscript.

Financial support for our work has been provided by the National Science Foundation, the Office of Naval Research, IBM, DEC, Xerox, and Siemens. We also wish to thank our home institutions, the University of Wisconsin–Madison and Cornell University, as well as the Institut National de Recherche en Informatique et en Automatique (INRIA) in Rocquencourt, France, where we were visiting researchers in 1982-83.

September 1988   Thomas W. Reps
                                                               Tim Teitelbaum

Contents

CHAPTER 1

Introduction

The Synthesizer Generator is a tool for implementing language-based editors. The editor designer prepares a specification that includes rules defining a language's context-free abstract syntax, context-sensitive relationships, display format, and concrete input syntax. From this specification, the Synthesizer Generator creates a display editor for manipulating objects according to these rules.

The Synthesizer Generator is especially well suited for creating editors that enforce the syntax and static semantics of a particular language. Each object to be edited is represented as a consistently attributed derivation tree. As one syntactically well-formed tree is changed into another, some of the attributes may no longer have consistent values; incremental analysis is performed by updating attribute values throughout the tree in response to each modification. If an editing operation modifies an object in such a way that context-dependent constraints are violated, the attributes that indicate satisfaction of constraints will receive new values; these attributes can annotate the display to provide the user with feedback about the existence of errors.

More generally, attributes may contain arbitrary auxiliary information, not merely error diagnostics. The collection of attributes constitutes a derived database of facts that can be presented on the screen and used to control the editing process.

Editor specifications are written in the Synthesizer Specification Language (SSL), which is built around the concepts of an *attribute grammar* and a type definition facility, although certain features are tailored to the application domain of language-based editors. The Synthesizer Generator has two components:

1) A translator that takes an SSL specification as input and produces various tables as output, and

2) An editor kernel that consists of an attributed-tree data-type and a driver for interactively manipulating attributed trees; the kernel takes input from the keyboard (and mouse) and executes appropriate operations on the current tree.

A shell program named sgen handles the details of invoking the translator and producing a language-based editor from the resulting tables.

Generated editors all follow the same editing paradigm. Although each has been customized for a particular language, every editor has the following similar characteristics.

Objects are contained in a collection of named *buffers*. Typically, each file being edited is read into a distinct buffer.

At any given moment, one or more buffers are displayed in *windows*. Each window shows the contents of a single buffer; the same buffer can be displayed in several windows. In general, only part of a buffer is visible in a window and the window is scrolled to shift the portion viewed. Separate windows associated with the same buffer may be scrolled to different regions of the buffer.

The objects contained in buffers are *terms*, *i.e.* derivation trees with respect to the underlying abstract syntax of the language. The nodes of a term are instances of *operators* and the subtrees of a node are the operator's *arguments*, themselves terms. Each term has a two-dimensional, textual *display representation*. The view of a term displayed in a window is a rectangular section of this textual representation.

Each buffer has a *selection*, the subterm or sublist of current interest. The selection, if visible within a window, is highlighted. Two means are provided for changing the position of the selection.

First, tree-walking commands, such as **forward-preorder**, **backward-preorder**, **forward-sibling**, **backward-sibling**, and **ascend-to-parent**, allow navigation according to the structure of the term. Such commands are usually bound to particular keys or key-sequences. In addition, they may be invoked by name or selected from a menu.

Second, the selection can be repositioned using a mouse or other locating device such as the cursor keys of an ASCII terminal. Clicking the mouse on a character causes the selection to change to the subterm associated with that character; dragging the mouse between two characters causes the selection to change to the smallest subterm or sublist containing both characters. Because the selection is a subterm of the buffer and not a substring of its output representation, the selection always denotes a syntactically well-formed constituent.

Each editing transaction replaces the selected subterm or sublist with another. Modifications are effected either by transformation, by command, or by text editing.

A *transformation* determines a replacement value for the selected subterm as a function of its current value. At any given moment, a transformation is either *enabled* or *disabled* depending on whether or not its *pattern* matches the value of the selection. Enabled transformations are listed in a menu and can be invoked either by name or by menu selection. Simple transformations replace one constant value with another. For example,

```
<statement>
```

might be replaced with

```
while <expression> do
    <statement>
```

More interesting transformations restructure the current selection. For example, a transformation implementing the distributive law of arithmetic might change the formula

```
a*(b+c)
```

into the algebraically equivalent formula

```
a*b+a*c
```

Alternatively, the code fragment

```
for i := 1 to n do
   write(i,i*i)
```

might be transformed into the computationally equivalent fragment

```
i := 1;
while i<=n do
   begin
      write(i,i*i);
      i := i+1
   end
```

Transformations cannot introduce context-free syntax errors, since their definitions are type-checked when the SSL specification is compiled into an editor.

Transformations are language dependent and differ from editor to editor, but *system commands* such as **cut-to-clipped** and **paste-from-clipped** are language independent and are provided with every generated editor. In typical text-based editors, the cut operation removes selected text and leaves an editing cursor positioned between two adjacent characters. By contrast, in our term-based editors, the cut operation replaces the selected subterm with another subterm known as a *placeholder*. For example, cutting

```
for i := 1 to n do
    write(i,i*i)
```

might replace the selection with

```
<statement>
```

As with transformations, cut-and-paste editing cannot introduce context-free syntax errors.

The textual display representation of the selection can be edited in the fashion of a typical screen-oriented text editor. The text is implicitly captured into a *text buffer* upon the first action that implies textual modification. The text buffer is then displayed on the screen in place of the selection, so its presence is barely perceptible. Within the text buffer, characters can be inserted and deleted arbitrarily. A *character selection*, identifying the location where text editing changes occur, can be repositioned by the usual two-dimensional cursor motions or by clicking a mouse or other locating device. When the term selection is directed away from its current location, the text is parsed with respect to the *concrete input syntax* corresponding to the current selection context. Syntax errors are pinpointed and must be corrected before proceeding. When syntactically correct, the characters contained in the text buffer are translated into a term, which then replaces the original selected subterm and is displayed according to its output representation. The visual effect may just be that the text appears to have been pretty-printed. Alternatively, the text may be translated to a term whose output representation is entirely different.

A term contained in a buffer is *attributed*, *i.e.* it is decorated with computed values that characterize the term. After each buffer modification, these attributes are updated so that, at all times, they form a consistent database of derived information. Selected attribute values may be displayed as part of the output representation of the term and provide immediate feedback to the user as editing progresses.

When editing is finished, buffer contents are written to files. The files may record either the abstract structure of terms or their textual display representations. A text file can be read back into a buffer only if the generated editor has been provided with a concrete input syntax for the entire language.

This manual describes Release 3.0 of the Synthesizer Generator. Chapter 2 discusses how editors are specified in SSL. Chapter 3 describes how to use an editor generated with the Synthesizer Generator. Chapter 4 concerns the SSL debugger. Chapter 5 outlines facilities for interfacing editors to code written in C. Appendix A contains a complete specification of a simple desk calculator. Portions of this specification are used throughout the manual to illustrate features of SSL. Appendix B, presented in the standard format for Unix-manual entries, documents how to invoke sgen to build an editor. Appendix C lists the commands available in an editor generated with the Synthesizer Generator. Appendix D describes workstation-specific information required for running an editor. Appendix E lists the demonstration editors that are included with the release of the Synthesizer Generator. Appendix F contains a context-free grammar for SSL.

CHAPTER 2

Specifying an Editor

This chapter defines SSL, the language in which editors are specified. Each SSL specification consists of a list of *declarations*. Although declarations may appear in any order, some kinds of symbols must be declared before they can be used.

The core of an editor specification for a given language is the definition of the language's abstract syntax, given as a set of grammar rules. The grammar rules are essentially productions of a context-free grammar. However, because the grammar is used to define abstract syntax, productions contain no terminal symbols.

The derivation trees derived from nonterminal symbols are known as *terms* and the set of terms derived from a given nonterminal symbol constitute a *phylum*. The grammar should be viewed as a type-definition mechanism in which the nonterminal symbols are type names and each nonterminal symbol, taken as a type name, denotes a set of values known as a phylum. We often refer to nonterminal symbols as phyla, although more precisely they are the names of phyla. Each production derives terms that can be thought of as *n*-ary records. The alternatives of a given nonterminal give rise to different record variants. Terms are used both as abstract representations of objects to be edited and as computational values. Each production has a name, known as an *operator*, that can be used in computational expressions (in different contexts) both as a record constructor and as a selector that discriminates between variants.

Productions, nonterminal symbols, and operator names are defined simultaneously in *phylum declarations*. A *root declaration* specifies the root nonterminal symbol of the grammar. During an editing session, buffers typically contain terms derived from the root symbol, and each editing transaction performs a subterm replacement within this term. *Property declarations* specify special properties of phyla such as whether they are optional elements or lists.

Syntax-directed computations on terms are specified by attribution rules. *Attribute declarations* associate attributes with nonterminals and productions. *Equation declarations* define the values of attributes in terms of other attributes that occur in the production. Common operations may be abstracted into functions by *function declarations*. The derivation trees contained in buffers during editing are fully attributed, *i.e.* all attributes of all nonterminals and productions are given values. Attribute values are updated automatically as objects are modified.

The display representation of the terms of a phylum is defined by *unparsing declarations* associated with each production. The concrete syntax so defined determines how objects are displayed on the screen. Display representations may, in part, be influenced by the values of attributes. Thus, after each editing transaction, correct attribute values are first reestablished and only then is the object redisplayed. Different manners of displaying terms are provided by *view declarations*; access to fonts of different sizes and characteristics is provided by *style declarations*.

Objects are modified by three sorts of editing transactions: text editing, structural transformation, and system command. The same system commands (*e.g.* for cut and paste) are provided with each generated editor; the system commands are described in Chapter 3. Text editing and transformations are defined by (editor-specific) declarations, as described below.

The structure of edited text and its translation to abstract form is determined by an input syntax. *Parsing declarations* define the productions of a grammar to be used for parsing text (*i.e.* the phylum of parse trees). Precedence and associativity of terminal symbols that may appear in parsing declarations can be defined in *precedence declarations*. The translation of text to abstract syntax is defined by attribution equations associated with the productions of the input syntax.

Only a subset of the input syntax is recognized at any given moment, according to the position of the selected subterm in the abstract syntax tree. *Entry declarations* define this correspondence between the abstract syntax of editable objects and subsets of the input syntax. Each well-formed text segment in a given context determines a parse tree with respect to the input syntax, which, in turn, is translated to a fragment of abstract syntax by attribution. Each text editing transaction has the net effect of replacing a piece of the edited object by a distinguished attribute of the root of the parse tree.

Transformation declarations specify how to restructure an object when the component located at the selected subterm matches a given structural pattern.

2.1. Lexical Matters

An *identifier* is a sequence of letters, digits, or underscore characters, beginning with a letter or an underscore. Upper- and lower-case letters are considered distinct characters. The following identifiers are reserved and may not be used for other purposes:

and	as	default	demand	end
exported	ext_computers	false	forall	foreign
in	inh	inherited	left	list
let	local	nil	nil_attr	nonassoc
on	optional	parse	prec	readonly
repeated	right	root	sparse	store
style	syn	synthesized	transform	true
typedef	unparse	view	with	

The file atoms.ssl is always prepended to source files processed with sgen. This prefix defines the primitive phyla listed in Section 2.2.1, the built-in functions listed in Section 2.5.3, and the phyla associated with text files, as described in Section 2.2.4. Identifiers BASEVIEW, WHITESPACE, and INITIAL are also predefined. Other identifiers defined in atoms.ssl begin with underscores. In order to avoid inadvertent collisions with them, it is recommended that user-declared identifiers not begin with an underscore. The identifiers declared in atoms.ssl are technically not reserved; they are merely predefined and may be redefined in local scopes. Identifiers of the form gen$i$, where i is an unsigned integer, are generated by the SSL compiler and should be avoided.

Blanks, tabs, and newlines in the specification file are ignored except that they serve to delimit tokens. Comments, delimited by /* and */, may appear before or after any token. Since the first */ after the beginning of a comment terminates the comment, comments within comments are not permitted. Comments may cross line boundaries.

Sgen, the standard shell script used for compiling editors, filters all source files through the C-preprocessor [Kernighan78]. Thus, macros, include files, and conditional compilation may be used within SSL source.

The consistent use of a fixed convention regarding the use of upper and lower case letters in identifiers is recommended, as it makes specifications more readable. One such convention, illustrated by the sample specification in Appendix A, is

lower_case	phyla of abstract syntax
CapitalizedWords	operators and functions
lower_case	attributes
CAPITALIZED	phyla of lexemes and phyla used for attribute types
CapitalizedWords	phyla of input syntax

One may wish to distinguish phyla of input syntax from operator and function names, for example, by using some unique prefix.

2.2. Phyla, Operators, and Terms

The concepts phylum, operator, and term are defined mutually recursively. A *phylum* is a set of terms. A *term* is the result of applying a k-ary operator to k terms of the appropriate phyla. A k-ary *operator* is a constructor-function mapping k terms to a term. Operators are typed; the result, as well as each argument position, has an associated phylum.

In editors, the objects created, modified, and destroyed by the user are terms. Values computed as attributes of these terms are themselves terms.

Each phylum contains a distinguished term known as its *completing term* and a distinguished term known as its *placeholder term*. The same term can be both the completing term and the placeholder term of a phylum. The role of these distinguished terms is explained in Section 2.2.3, "List phyla, optional phyla, and placeholder terms" and in Section 3.11, "Structural Editing."

Example 2.2(a). Let us consider a phylum of binary trees, TREE. Associated with TREE are two operators: Leaf (of arity 0), and Node (of arity 2, with parameter phyla TREE and TREE). TREE can be defined inductively as follows:

1) The term Leaf() is in TREE;
2) If t_1 and t_2 are terms in TREE, then the term Node(t_1,t_2) is in TREE;
3) No other terms are in TREE.

Phylum TREE is the infinite collection of terms

```
{
Leaf(),
Node(Leaf(),Leaf()),
Node(Node(Leaf(),Leaf()),Leaf()),
Node(Leaf(),Node(Leaf(),Leaf())),
  . . .

}
```

As completing and placeholder term, we might choose the simplest term: Leaf(). An SSL specification for this phylum is given in Example 2.2.2(a).

2.2.1. Primitive phyla

Primitive phyla contain terms that cannot be further decomposed in SSL. The following primitive phyla are predefined:

Phylum	Terms
BOOL	Truth values
INT	Integers
REAL	Floating-point numbers
CHAR	Characters
STR	Character strings
PTR	References to SSL values
ATTR	References to attributes
TABLE[α]	Hash tables
MAP[α,β]	Maps

There are two categories of primitive phyla: *unparameterized* and *parameterized*. An unparameterized phylum is just a set of terms, as described in Section 2.2. For example, BOOL is a phylum consisting of truth values, INT is a phylum consisting of signed whole numbers, *etc*. Technically, a parameterized phylum is not a single phylum, but is a family of phyla. For each substitution of phyla for parameters, there is a distinct phylum instance in the family. For example, MAP[α,β] is a predefined parameterized phylum, with parameters α and β. Each of the following is an instance of the parameterized phylum MAP:

MAP[STR,INT]
MAP[STR,STR]
MAP[STR,MAP[STR,INT]]

Special syntax is provided in SSL for denoting the terms of primitive phyla, often referred to as *constants*. For example, the truth values of phylum BOOL are denoted by true and false, the integers in phylum INT are denoted by 0, 1, 2, *etc*. The syntax of these primitive constants is summarized in the table given in Figure 2.1. For each primitive phylum, the placeholder term is the same as the phylum's completing term.

Some primitive values do not have corresponding constant denotations. For example, there is no SSL constant corresponding to negative one, since −1 is an expression — the negation function applied to positive one. On the other hand, some primitive values have more than one denotation. For example, integer denotations beginning with 0 are taken to be octal numerals. Thus, the unsigned integer constants 8, 010, 0010 each denote the integer eight.

Phylum	Terms	Constants	Completing term
BOOL	false, true	false, true	false
INT	integers	0, 01, 02, ... (octal) 1, 2, 3, ... (decimal)	0
REAL	single-precision floating-point numbers	0.0, 0e0, 0.0e0 123.45e−6	0.0e0
CHAR	8-bit characters	'a', 'b', ..., 'A', 'B', ... '0', '1', '2', ... '!', '%', '#', ... '\n', '\r', '\b', '\t' '\'', '\"', '\\' '\000', '\001', ...	'\000'
STR	Sequences of CHARs. All CHARs except '\000' permitted.	"" "ab...AB...01...!%..." "\n\r\b\t\f\'\"\\" "\001\002\003..."	""
PTR	References to values	nil	nil
ATTR	References to attributes	nil_attr	nil_attr
TABLE[α]	Hash Tables	*no constants*	*undefined*
MAP[α,β]	Maps	*no constants*	*undefined*

Figure 2.1. Syntax of constants of primitive phyla.

The backslash symbol is used as an escape character in constants of type
CHAR and STR. The meaning of escape sequences is as follows:

Escape sequence	Meaning
\n	newline
\r	return
\b	backspace
\t	tab
\'	single-quote
\"	double-quote
\\	backslash
\000	octal 0
\001	octal 1
. . .	. . .

If c is any character other than one of those shown in the table above, \c just
denotes the character c itself.

Built-in operations on primitive phyla are defined in Section 2.5.3, "Operations on primitive phyla" and Section 2.5.5, "Relational operations." Unparsing
rules for values of primitive phyla appear in Section 2.6.3, "Formatting the
display representation." The declaration of new primitive phyla is described in
Section 5.2.

The symbols *phylum-name* and *phylum* are used throughout this manual in the
description of SSL's syntax. A *phylum-name* is an identifier that denotes a single phylum. For example, BOOL, INT, and TREE are *phylum-names* but MAP
is not. A *phylum* is either a *phylum-name* or it is an instance of a parameterized
phylum. For example, the phylum instance MAP[STR,INT] is a *phylum*. In
addition, within the scope of a forall, the quantified phylum names of the forall
are considered phyla. For example, within the scope of forall alpha in . . . end,
MAP[alpha,alpha] is a *phylum*, as is alpha itself. The name of a parameterized
phylum, without arguments, is neither a *phylum-name* nor a *phylum*.

2.2.2. User-defined phyla and operators

New phyla and operators are declared in terms of other phyla or recursively in
terms of themselves. There are two kinds of *phylum declarations*: productions
and lexemes.

Productions

A *production declaration* defines a new operator and includes all terms constructible by that operator in a given phylum. The form of a production declaration is

> *phylum-name* : *operator-name* (*phylum*$_1$ *phylum*$_2$ $\cdots$ *phylum*$_k$) ;

The phylum named by *phylum-name* is referred to as the *left-hand-side phylum*. Phyla *phylum*$_1$, . . . , *phylum*$_k$ are known as the *parameters* of the operator. A production declares that all terms constructed by applying k-ary operator *operator-name* to argument terms of phyla *phylum*$_1$, . . . , *phylum*$_k$ are members of the left-hand-side phylum. An operator may not be associated with more than one phylum. The operator name, an identifier, is optional; if omitted, a generated operator name of the form gen$i$, for some integer i, is assigned. Operator names in productions are usually not omitted.

Two varieties of factoring support abbreviation of phylum declarations. First, a collection of operators can be declared with a single parenthesized list of parameters; all operators are thereby declared to have the same arity and parameter phyla. Second, if the left-hand-side phyla of consecutive declarations are the same, the name can be factored to the left and the operators and parameters listed as alternatives separated by a vertical bar. These two abbreviations can be combined; thus, a more general syntax of phylum declarations is

> *phylum-name* :
>   *operator-name*, . . . , *operator-name* (*parameters*)
> | *operator-name*, . . . , *operator-name* (*parameters*)
>   . . .
> | *operator-name*, . . . , *operator-name* (*parameters*)
>   ;

Productions with the same left-hand-side phylum need not be grouped consecutively in the specification. This feature allows specifications of separate aspects of a language to be placed in separate portions of a specification. (See Section 2.9, "Support for Modular Specifications.")

Determination of completing and placeholder terms for a user-defined phylum depends on whether the phylum has an associated property declaration. For phyla without property declarations, the completing and placeholder terms are defined in terms of the first declared operator of the phylum, as follows: a phylum's completing term is the term constructed by applying the first operator of the phylum to the completing terms of its parameter phyla. The completing term of a phylum must not be circularly defined. The placeholder term (of a phylum without property declarations) is the same as its completing term. For the definition of the completing and placeholder terms of phyla with property declarations, see Section 2.2.3, "List phyla, optional phyla, and placeholders."

Example 2.2.2(a). The following SSL phylum declaration defines phylum TREE, as described in Example 2.2(a):

```
TREE:  Leaf()
  | Node(TREE TREE)
  ;
```

Example 2.2.2(b). The following phylum declaration (from Appendix A) defines phylum exp, a phylum of arithmetic expressions with integer leaves:

```
/*  11 */     exp: Null()
/*  12 */        | Sum, Diff, Prod, Quot(exp  exp)
/*  13 */        | Const(INT)
/*  14 */        ;
```

The completing term and the placeholder term of phylum exp is the term Null().

Example 2.2.2(c). The following declarations (from Appendix A) define phyla ENV and BINDING. ENV consists of right-recursive lists of zero or more BINDINGs. BINDING consists of ID-INT pairs. Phylum ID, a phylum of identifiers, is assumed to be declared elsewhere (for example, as in Example 2.2.2(g)).

```
/* 110 */     ENV: NullEnv()
/* 111 */        | EnvConcat( BINDING ENV )
/* 112 */        ;
/* 113 */     BINDING: Binding( ID INT );
```

Example 2.2.2(d). The following declaration illustrates that the parameters of a user-declared phylum can be instances of a parameterized phylum:

```
PAIR: Pair(INT MAP[STR,STR]);
```

Lexemes

A *lexical phylum* is a set of strings defined by one or more regular expressions. For the purpose of lexical analysis (described in Section 2.7), lexical phyla are considered subphyla of STR, the predefined primitive phylum consisting of all possible strings. An input string recognized by the scanner as a member of a given lexical phylum is necessarily one of the strings in the phylum. For all other purposes, *e.g.* phylum definition and type checking, a lexical phylum is synonymous with STR. In particular, the value of a variable with a lexical phylum as its type is not guaranteed to be one of the strings in the phylum and may be any string whatsoever.

The form of a *lexeme declaration* is

> *phylum-name* : *lexeme-name* <   *regular-expression* > ;

It declares that all strings generated by the given *regular-expression* are in the named phylum. The regular expression must be separated from the closing angle bracket by at least one blank. It must itself contain no embedded blank characters other than those explicitly escaped by a backslash. The *lexeme-name* is used in the definition of the concrete input grammar, as described in Section 2.7. As with operator names in productions, the lexeme name is optional; if omitted, a generated name of the form gen$i$, for some integer i, is assigned. The lexeme name is usually omitted from a lexeme declaration.

With few exceptions, the regular expressions permitted are exactly the regular expressions accepted by the UNIX lexical analyzer generator lex [Lesk75]. In the following table, c stands for any printable character, n stands for any decimal integer, and e stands for any regular expression. Each of the following is a regular expression:

Expression	Meaning
c	the character c
$"c_1c_2c_3"$	the string $c_1c_2c_3$
$\backslash c$	the character c
$[c_1c_2c_3]$	the character c_1, c_2, or c_3
$[c_1-c_2]$	any of the characters from c_1 through c_2
$[\hat{}c_1c_2c_3]$	any character but c_1, c_2, and c_3
.	any character but newline
$\hat{}e$	an e at the beginning of a line
$e\$$	an e at the end of a line
$e?$	an optional e
e^*	0 or more instances of e
$e+$	1 or more instances of e
e_1e_2	an e_1 followed by an e_2
$e_1\|e_2$	an e_1 or an e_2
(e)	an e
e_1/e_2	an e_1 but only if followed by e_2
$e\{n_1,n_2\}$	n_1 through n_2 occurrences of e

The symbols

$$" \ \backslash \ [\ ] \ - \ \hat{} \ . \ \$ \ ? \ * \ + \ | \ (\ ) \ / \ \{ \ \} \ \% \ < \ >$$

each have reserved meaning in regular expressions. When used as literal text characters, they either should be escaped with a backslash or should appear within quotation marks. Within square brackets, however, only four characters have special meaning: \, −, ^, and blank. Any other characters within square brackets denote themselves.

Exceptions from lex are as follows:

1) The blank character within square brackets must be escaped.
2) Definitions, as described in Section 6 of the lex manual [Lesk75], are not supported.
3) Left-context sensitivity is supported in a nonstandard way. In particular, the regular expression may optionally be preceded and/or followed by a state name enclosed in angle brackets. This feature is described in Section 2.7.5, "Lexical analysis."

Lexeme declarations are not totally independent; rather, they form an ordered list. During lexical analysis in a running editor, this order influences the recognition process. In particular, when more than one regular expression matches a string, the longest match is made; when several rules match the same number of characters, the declaration that comes earliest in the specification is used. Thus, for example, all keyword definitions should precede a definition for a class of identifiers. Because of this order dependence, it is recommended that all lexeme declarations be kept together in a separate file so that the sequence is evident.

The distinguished phylum WHITESPACE is used to define how the system should recognize whitespace when parsing concrete input syntax. (Whitespace characters are ignored during parsing; see Section 2.7.5, "Lexical analysis.")

As with production declarations, when several lexeme declarations are associated with the same phylum, the phylum can be factored to the left and the lexeme declarations listed as alternatives separated by vertical bars:

```
phylum-name :
    lexeme-name <  regular-expression  >
  | lexeme-name <  regular-expression  >
    . . .
  | lexeme-name <  regular-expression  >
  ;
```

Mixing productions and lexemes as alternatives of the same phylum is not permitted.

Example 2.2.2(e). The phylum of unsigned decimal integer denotations is defined by the lexeme declaration

/* 47 */   INTEGER: < [0–9]+ >;

Example 2.2.2(f). The keyword let is defined to be the one element of the singleton phylum LET

/* 94 */   LET: < "let" >;

Example 2.2.2(g). A phylum of identifiers can be defined by the lexeme declaration

/* 97 */   ID: < [a–zA–Z][a–zA–Z0–9]* >;

Example 2.2.2(h). Ordinarily, blank, newline, and tab characters are considered whitespace:

```
/* 48 */      WHITESPACE: < [\ \n\t] >;
```

Example 2.2.2(i). To recognize the let keyword in either lower or upper case, either of the following two declarations would be correct. However, due to an idiosyncrasy of an optimization phase of the Synthesizer Generator, the first is likely to yield a more space-efficient scanner.

```
LET:     < "let" >
  |      < "LET" >
  ;
```

```
LET:     < "let"|"LET" >;
```

Example 2.2.2(j). The desk calculator of Appendix A contains declarations

```
/* 97 */      ID: < [a–zA–Z][a–zA–Z0–9]* >;
/* 113 */     BINDING: Binding( ID INT );
```

and, on line 123, the constant Binding("?",0). Note that the regular expression for ID does not generate "?". Nonetheless, Binding("?",0) is type-correct because, for the purposes of defining phyla and checking types, ID is identical to STR.

The SSL compiler uses lex to create a scanner. Occasionally, a moderate collection of lexeme declarations causes one of lex's fixed-size tables to overflow. To enlarge these tables, prepare a file containing lines of the form

```
%x nnn
```

where *nnn* is a decimal integer representing the size parameter and *x* selects the table as follows:

An appropriate display representation for the four productions would be the null string, <answer>, yes, and no, respectively. (See Section 2.6, "View and Unparsing Declarations.")

List phyla

The convention that all insertions take place at placeholders leads to the notion that, in a list, a placeholder may appear before and after every list item. Each of these "between-item" placeholders is implicitly optional; *i.e.* they are inserted when selected and removed as the selection is moved away. A phylum is declared to have this behavior by the list and **optional list** property declarations. In addition, for any list phylum, the user will be able to make selections of sub-lists.

A list phylum must have exactly two productions — one nullary, the other binary and right recursive.

When a command such as **forward-with-optionals** is used to advance the selection through a list, placeholders before and after every nonempty list item are first inserted and then removed. When a list of n items contains a place-holder for a new $(n+1)$st item, it is actually a list of $n+1$ items, one of which is the placeholder term of the given item phylum.

The only difference between a list phylum and an optional list phylum con-cerns the behavior of placeholders for empty lists. Optional list phyla are treated as lists of length 0 or more: if the selection is moved away from the placeholder term of an empty list, it reverts to the completing term. By contrast, non-optional list phyla are treated as lists of length 1 or more: the placeholder term remains until at least one item has been inserted into the list.

The completing terms and placeholder terms of list phyla are defined as fol-lows:

The completing term of a non-optional list phylum is the singleton list con-structed by applying the binary production to the completing term of its left parameter phylum and to the list's nullary term. The placeholder term of a non-optional list phylum is the same as its completing term.

The completing term of an optional list phylum is the constant term con-structed from the nullary production. The placeholder term of an optional list is constructed exactly as if the phylum had not been declared to be optional; that is, the placeholder term is the singleton list constructed by applying the list's binary production to the completing term of its left param-eter phylum and to the list's nullary term.

Letter	Table selected
p	positions
n	states
e	tree nodes
a	transitions
k	packed character classes
o	output array size

Use the −L *filename* flag of sgen to cause these parameters to be passed to lex. Lex prints out table sizes, both limits and the amount used, whenever any parameter has been set. Thus, the first time a table overflows, the current table limits can be determined by recompiling with some arbitrary parameter setting. Double all parameters until the compilation succeeds, and then scale back appropriately.

2.2.3. List phyla, optional phyla, and placeholder terms

In the editing paradigm supported by generated editors, insertions may be made when the selection is a *placeholder term*. Typically, the unparsing of a place-holder term is a phrase or metasymbol describing the class of objects that can be inserted at the given location. Structured placeholders with subcomponents are also permitted. The term being "inserted" actually replaces the placeholder term in the edited object. The inverse operation, "deleting" a component of a term, replaces the given component with the appropriate placeholder term.

A *property declaration* specifies the special phylum properties *optional* and *list*. These properties influence the manner in which terms of the phylum are edited. For example, a list phylum is treated as a linear list of items; before the list, between any two items of the list, and after the list, another item can be inserted. When the selection is advanced to such an insertion point in a list, a placeholder appears; when the selection moves away from the insertion point, the placeholder disappears. Similarly, placeholders for optional phyla appear and disappear as the selection is advanced through a term. When the selection is advanced to a currently unexpanded optional phylum, a placeholder for the phy-lum appears; if the selection moves away without any insertion having been made, the placeholder disappears.

In addition to the special editing properties of list phyla, SSL provides built-in operators for manipulating lists. See Section 2.5.4, "List operations," for the details of these operations.

Property declarations have one of the following three forms:

```
list phylum₁, . . . , phylumₖ ;
optional phylum₁, . . . , phylumₖ ;
optional list phylum₁, . . . , phylumₖ ;
```

Unqualified (i.e. non-optional, non-list) phyla

For all phyla that are not declared with the qualifiers optional or list, there is no distinction between the phylum's placeholder term and the phylum's completing term; *i.e.* the placeholder term *is* the completing term.

Example 2.2.3(a). Recall the definition of phylum exp from Appendix A:

```
/* 11 */      exp: Null()
/* 12 */          | Sum, Diff, Prod, Quot(exp  exp)
/* 13 */          | Const(INT)
/* 14 */          ;
```

The placeholder term, as well as the completing term, for phylum exp is the term Null(). The display representation for exp is defined (on lines 30-37 of Appendix A) so that Null appears as <exp> and Sum is displayed parenthesized with a plus sign between the two operands. Thus, the term Sum(Null(),Null()) is displayed as

(<exp> + <exp>)

Insertion of a particular expression at either of the <exp> placeholders is accomplished by replacement of the corresponding Null() subterm.

Optional phyla

For syntactic components that are optional and usually omitted it is inappropriate to employ placeholders that remain on the screen until a component has been filled in — the screen would quickly become cluttered, and, what is worse, there would be no way to make them go away. In such cases, it is better to have placeholders that appear on the screen only when selected. This effect is obtained by distinguishing between the placeholder term of a phylum (which is given a visible display representation) and the completing term (which is given a null display representation).

The qualifier optional specifies that whenever the selection is [a] completing term, the completing term is automatically replaced by [a] placeholder term. Symmetrically, whenever the selection moves a[way] placeholder term of a phylum qualified as optional, the placeh[older] automatically replaced by the completing term.

Some selection-motion commands, *e.g.* forward-preorder, a[lways] skip over the completing terms of optional phyla. Thus, if such [a command is] used to advance through an object, optional phyla will not be app[arent. In con]trast, other selection-motion commands, *e.g.* forward-with-opt[ional,] completing terms of optional phyla. Thus, traversing an object w[ith a com]mand causes each encountered completing term for an optiona[l phylum to be] first replaced by a placeholder term and then to be restored to [the completing] term. (See Section 3.6, "Changing the Structural Selection by [Moving the] Edited Term.")

Placeholders for optional phyla can also appear as the result [of a transforma]tion. This will occur if the transformation explicitly constructs a [term] that contains a placeholder. "Templates" inserted by transforma[tions often] display optional placeholders. Such a placeholder will rema[in visible] until it is selected and then the selection is changed. Also, tra[nsformations can] be written to reveal optional placeholders once they have d[isappeared. (See] Section 2.8, "Transformation Declarations.")

The placeholder term and the completing term of an optio[nal phy]lum are determined as follows. An optional (non-list) phy[lum may have any] number of productions, but one of them must be a nullary pr[oduction. The com]pleting term is the term constructed from this nullary product[ion. If the phylum] has more than one nullary production, the completing term [is constructed from the] first nullary production of the phylum that appears in the [declaration.] The placeholder term is the term constructed by "completin[g" the produc]tion of the phylum that is not the aforementioned completing [term.]

Example 2.2.3(b). The following declaration defines [the phylum] answer. The completing term is NoPrompt() and the [placeholder is] Prompt().

```
optional answer;
answer: NoPrompt()
  | Prompt()
  | Yes()
  | No()
  ;
```

Example 2.2.3(c). Assume that phylum exp is declared as in Example 2.2.3(a). Then the following rules define calc to be a list phylum consisting of lists of exp terms:

```
/*  7 */      list calc;
/*  8 */      calc: CalcNil()
/*  9 */          | CalcPair(exp calc)
/*  10 */         ;
```

Since phylum calc is a non-optional list, its completing term is the same as its placeholder term: CalcPair(Null(), CalcNil()). If, instead, calc were declared to be an optional list, then its completing term would be CalcNil() and its place-holder term would be CalcPair(Null(), CalcNil()).

2.2.4. Predefined non-primitive phyla

Phyla textfile and textline are predefined in atoms.ssl, as follows:

```
list textfile;
textfile: TextFileNil( )
    |       TextFilePair( textline textfile )
    ;
textline: TextLineNil( )
    |       TextLine( STR )
    ;
```

A textfile is a list of zero or more strings that are displayed on consecutive lines. By virtue of the list declaration, a placeholder is always displayed for an empty textfile. The display form of this placeholder, as defined in atoms.ssl, is <text>. User-specified phyla can incorporate textfile constituents. Many built-in system commands store textual output in buffers. Such a buffer contains a term of phylum textfile.

2.2.5. Root declaration

Every SSL specification must have one *root declaration* that declares the phy-lum of editable objects. A root declaration has the form

> root *phylum* ;

By default, new buffers are given the phylum specified in the root declaration. In addition, as described in Section 2.5.1, "Variables," the meaning of upward remote attribute sets depends upon this phylum.

2.3. Attribute Declarations and Attribute Equations

Context-dependent features of a language can be described in an editor-specification using attributes and attribute equations in the style of an attribute grammar. An attribute grammar extends a context-free grammar by attaching attributes to the symbols of the grammar [Knuth68]. Associated with each production of the grammar is a set of equations; each equation defines one attribute as the value of an expression defined in terms of other attributes accessible within the production.

2.3.1. Attribute declarations

Attributes may be associated either with phyla or with productions. Those associated with productions are known as *local attributes* and are discussed later in this section.

Attributes associated with phyla are divided into two disjoint classes: *synthesized* attributes and *inherited* attributes. Attributes are attached to a phylum by an *attribute declaration* that specifies the name of the phylum, the type of each attribute (some phylum), and whether each attribute is synthesized or inherited. The form of an attribute declaration is

> $phylum_0$ {
>   synthesized $phylum_1$ attribute-name$_1$;
>   . . .
>   inherited $phylum_k$ attribute-name$_k$;
>   } ;

The attribute names of a phylum are in a separate name space associated with the phylum; different phyla can have attributes with the same name. Declarations of synthesized and inherited attributes may be freely intermixed; synthesized attributes do not have to precede declarations of inherited attributes.

The keywords synthesized and inherited may be abbreviated as syn and inh, respectively.

An attribute's type can be either a built-in phylum or a user-defined phylum. Because precisely the same sort of rules are used to define attribute types and abstract syntax, the abstract-syntax tree being edited and the attributes attached to it are all elements in the universe of terms. A given term, in different contexts, may be both an attribute value and a piece of the abstract syntax of an object being edited.

It is not necessary that all attributes of a phylum be grouped within a single attribute declaration; additional attributes can be declared in subsequent attribute declarations for the phylum. (See Section 2.9, "Support for Modular Specifications.")

Example 2.3.1(a). The following attribute declaration (from Appendix A) associates with phylum exp a synthesized attribute v of type INT:

/* 17 */   exp {synthesized INT v;};

Phylum INT is the predefined primitive phylum of integers. The attribute equations of the desk calculator (not shown here) define attribute exp.v to be the arithmetic value of expression exp.

Example 2.3.1(b). The following attribute declaration (from Appendix A) associates with phylum exp an inherited attribute env of type ENV:

/* 130 */   exp {inherited ENV env;};

Phylum ENV is a user-defined phylum containing environments of name-value bindings; its declaration, on lines 83-85 of Appendix A, is explained in Example 2.2.2(c). The attribute equations of the desk calculator (not shown here) define attribute exp.env to be the environment of name-value bindings in which the instance of expression exp occurs.

Example 2.3.1(c). The following attribute declaration (from Appendix A) associates with phylum exp an inherited attribute env of type MAP[ID,INT]:

/* 130A */   exp {inherited MAP[ID,INT] env;};

Phylum MAP[ID,INT], an instance of the predefined parameterized phylum MAP[α,β], contains finite functions mapping identifiers to integers. The attribute equations of the alternative version of the desk calculator (not shown here) define attribute exp.env to be the environment of name-value bindings in which expression exp occurs.

Whereas synthesized and inherited attributes are associated with phyla, *local attributes* are associated with productions. A local attribute declaration resembles the declaration of a synthesized or inherited attribute and has the form

local *phylum attribute-name* ;

where *phylum* is the type of the attribute and *attribute-name* is its name. Local attribute declarations appear among a production's attribute equations, rather than among a phylum's attribute declarations. (See Section 2.3.2, "Attribute equations.") The local attributes of a production are in a separate name space from the local attributes of other productions.

Example 2.3.1(d). In Example 2.3.2(a), a local attribute is declared at the same time as its defining equation is given. In isolation, this declaration would appear as

```
exp: Quot {
   local STR error;
   };
```

which declares local attribute error of type STR associated with production Quot of phylum exp.

An attribute may be specified to be a *demand attribute*, which means that it is given a value only when necessary, *i.e.* only when its value is referenced, rather than being automatically maintained whether or not its value is needed. A reference to attribute a arises either directly from a need to display a on the screen or indirectly from the need to evaluate another attribute that depends on a. Demand attributes may be arguments of regular attributes and vice versa.

Individual demand attributes are specified by prefacing the declaration with the keyword demand.

demand synthesized *phylum attribute-name* ;
demand inherited *phylum attribute-name* ;
demand local *phylum attribute-name* ;

Alternatively, all attributes appearing in a specification can be made demand attributes by invoking sgen with the −d flag (see Appendix B). Note that the demand qualifier is a directive for the generated editor that affects only the efficiency of incremental evaluation; the values of attributes are unaffected. See [Reps83] or [Reps84] for a discussion of the details of the two approaches to incremental attribute evaluation. The relative merits of demand evaluation versus the default approach are application dependent.

2.3.2. Attribute equations

The values of attributes are defined by equation schemes given on a production-by-production basis. In production

phylum-name : *operator-name* (*phylum*$_1$ *phylum*$_2$ $\cdots$ *phylum*$_k$) ;

the synthesized attributes of *phylum-name*, the inherited attributes of *phylum*$_1$, ..., *phylum*$_k$, and the local attributes of the production are termed the production's *output attributes*. An *attribute equation* defines the value of an output attribute as a function of other attributes accessible within the production. The attribute equations of the production are grouped within curly braces in a declaration of the form

```
phylum-name : operator-name {
    output-attribute = expression ;
    . . .
    output-attribute = expression ;
    } ;
```

Any *expression* can appear on the right-hand side of an attribute equation provided its type matches the type of the given output attribute. (See Section 2.5, "Expressions.")

Declarations of local attributes may be freely intermixed with the production's equations; however, a local-attribute declaration must precede all uses of the attribute in expressions.

```
phylum-name : operator-name {
    local phylum attribute-name ;
    . . .
    output-attribute = expression ;
    . . .
    } ;
```

An output attribute b of a phylum X in a production is denoted by $X.b$. If the production contains more than one occurrence of a phylum X, then the different occurrences of b are denoted (from left to right) by $X\$1.b$, $X\$2.b$, etc. If b is an attribute of the left-hand-side phylum of the production, it can be denoted by $\$\$.b$. A local attribute b is just denoted by b.

Output attributes are examples of variables, as described in Section 2.5.1. Note that although each output attribute is a variable, the converse is not true. In particular, phylum occurrences and upward remote attribute sets are variables that may not appear on the left-hand side of attribute equations.

The attribute equations of an editor specification must obey the following two constraints:

1) *Well-formedness.* There must be exactly one equation for every output attribute of each production. The SSL translator will refuse to generate an editor from a specification that violates this condition.

2) *Noncircularity.* It must not be possible to build a derivation tree in which attributes are defined circularly. Whether or not the SSL translator tests a grammar for noncircularity depends upon which attribute-evaluation scheme is used.

As is the case with phylum declarations, two varieties of factoring support abbreviation of equation declarations. First, if several of a phylum's operators have identical equations, the equation declaration may contain a list of operators, thereby defining equations for several attributes simultaneously. Second, if the left-hand-side phyla of consecutive declarations are the same, the phylum can be factored to the left, and the operators and equations listed as alternatives separated by a vertical bar. The two abbreviations can be combined; the syntax of attribute equations is

---

phylum-name :

      operator-name, . . . , *operator-name* { *equations* }

   | *operator-name*, . . . , *operator-name* { *equations* }

   . . .

   | *operator-name*, . . . , *operator-name* { *equations* }

   ;

Attribute-equation declarations must follow the declaration of the production with which they are associated. However, productions and equations can be declared simultaneously, using the following syntax:

---

phylum-name :

      operator-name, . . . , *operator-name* (*parameters*) { *equations* }

   | *operator-name*, . . . , *operator-name* (*parameters*) { *equations* }

   . . .

   | *operator-name*, . . . , *operator-name* (*parameters*) { *equations* }

   ;

It is not necessary for the equations of every output attribute of a production to appear in one group. Rather, equations can be grouped logically according to their function. (See Section 2.9, "Support for Modular Specifications.")

Example 2.3.2(a). The following equations illustrate the use of synthesized and local attributes in the desk calculator of Appendix A. Assume that an INT attribute v of phylum exp has been declared. We define attribute v of each exp term to be the arithmetic value of the term. To do so, we use the v attributes of the subterms. Note, in the production exp:Const(INT), that exp.v is defined to be INT, the integer subterm of Const, *i.e.* a piece of the syntax tree being attributed. The local attribute error of Quot is defined to be either "<—DIVISION BY ZERO—>" or the null string, depending on whether or not the divisor is zero.

```
/* 18 */    exp: Null { exp.v = 0; }
/* 19 */      | Sum  { exp$1.v = exp$2.v + exp$3.v; }
/* 20 */      | Diff   { exp$1.v = exp$2.v – exp$3.v; }
/* 21 */      | Prod  { exp$1.v = exp$2.v * exp$3.v; }
/* 22 */      | Quot  { local STR error;
/* 23 */          error = (exp$3.v==0) ? "<—DIVISION BY ZERO—>" : "";
/* 24 */          exp$1.v = (exp$3.v==0) ? exp$2.v : (exp$2.v / exp$3.v) ;
/* 25 */          }
/* 26 */      | Const{ exp$1.v = INT; }
/* 27 */      ;
```

Example 2.3.2(b). The following equations illustrate the use of inherited attributes; they pass attribute env, an environment of name-value bindings, to each operand of a Sum, Diff, Prod, or Quot operator. Note the factoring that permits these equations to be defined for all four operations simultaneously.

```
/* 135 */    exp:
  . . .
/* 147 */    Sum, Diff, Prod, Quot {
/* 148 */        exp$2.env = exp$1.env;
/* 149 */        exp$3.env = exp$1.env;
/* 150 */        }
/* 151 */        ;
```

2.3.3. Attribute evaluation schemes

Three evaluation schemes are supported: UNORDERED, ORDERED, and ATO. The default scheme is ORDERED. An alternative evaluator may be selected by using the sgen flag –kernel *evaluation-scheme*.

UNORDERED

The UNORDERED evaluation scheme is Reps's original attribute-updating algorithm [Reps82]. It applies to arbitrary noncircular attribute grammars. If the UNORDERED evaluator is selected, the grammar is not checked to ensure that it is noncircular. If the grammar is circular, the generated editor may loop endlessly as it tries to update attribute values in the syntax tree. A circularity test is performed if the sgen flag –K is used. The UNORDERED evaluator is not recommended.

ORDERED

The ORDERED evaluation scheme is an incremental version of Kastens's attribute-evaluation algorithm [Kastens80, Reps88]. If the ORDERED evaluation scheme is selected, the SSL translator tests the grammar for "orderedness," a condition that is sufficient to guarantee that a grammar is noncircular. Most attribute grammars arising in practice are ordered. The editor designer will occasionally find that a grammar fails the test; however, this usually indicates the existence of an error in the specification.

A grammar can fail to be ordered in one of three ways, due to circularities that are detected after various steps of Kastens's algorithm for constructing attribute-evaluation tables. These errors are reported as being circularities of type 1, 2, and 3, respectively. A type 1 circularity indicates a circularity in the dependences of an individual production. A type 2 circularity indicates a circularity in the approximation of the productions' transitive dependences that the algorithm computes. A type 3 circularity indicates a circularity induced by the dependences that are added between attribute partitions. (For more details about circularities that arise during the Kastens construction, the reader is referred to [Kastens80] or Chapter 12 of [Reps88].)

Readers should understand that the Kastens algorithm is pessimistic, in the sense that a type 2 circularity does not necessarily indicate that a grammar is circular. All grammars that are circular will be reported to have either type 1 or type 2 circularities; however, some noncircular grammars will also be reported as having type 2 circularities.

A type 3 circularity indicates that the grammar is definitely not circular, but indicates a failure of Kastens's method for constructing attribute-grammar evaluators (due to certain approximations made during the construction). Perhaps the most common way type 3 circularities arise is to write a grammar in which there are two disjoint threadings of attribute dependences through the same productions, one threaded left-to-right and the other threaded right-to-left; such a grammar is noncircular but has a type 3 circularity. When type 3 circularities arise, it is often possible to work around the approximations made during the orderedness test by adding additional dependences to the specification that do not change its meaning. One way to accomplish this is by using attribute equations that have a conditional expression whose condition is true; attributes that appear in the "else" branch of the conditional introduce attribute dependences, but can never contribute to the attribute equation's value.

If the selected evaluation scheme is ORDERED and the specification fails the orderedness test, an editor will not be generated. We recommend changing the grammar to be ordered, rather than switching to the UNORDERED scheme.

ATO

Approximate Topological Ordering [Hoover87] is an attribute-evaluation method that has proven to be efficient in practice, although it is not guaranteed to be optimal in the sense of [Reps82]. ATO is Hoover's implementation of this method.

ATO offers two principal advantages. First, it works for any noncircular attribute grammar. Second, it is often faster than the other evaluators due to its special implementation of MAP-valued attributes. Two different implementations of maps are available: AVL and COLLECTIONS. While AVL can be used with all evaluators, COLLECTIONS are unique to ATO. AVL is the default under all evaluation schemes. If the evaluation scheme is ATO, the COLLECTIONS implementation of maps can be selected using the sgen −b flag.

COLLECTIONS impose some restrictions on the use of maps. In general, however, we believe that the speed advantages of COLLECTIONS outweigh the disadvantages of these limitations. The restrictions are as follows:

1) Phyla cannot contain maps as constituents.
2) The map-constructing operations (empty-map, initialized-map, single-point-update, and multiple-point-update) cannot be used in functions.
3) Certain map-valued expressions (to be described below) evaluate to *readonly* map values. A readonly map cannot be an argument to the map-updating operations single-point-update and multiple-point-update. In addition, an attribute can be equated to a readonly value only if the attribute has been declared readonly, as described in Appendix F. A map-valued expression is readonly except in one of the following three cases: (i) its outermost operation is a map-constructor, (ii) it is an attribute not declared readonly, (iii) it is an upward remote attribute reference that cannot resolve to a readonly attribute. Examples of expressions producing readonly values include function applications, conditional expressions, and readonly attributes.
4) Relational operations on maps are not available.
5) Map-valued attributes cannot be demand attributes.
6) All maps are displayed as [MAP].

If the ATO evaluator is selected, the grammar is not checked to ensure that it is noncircular. If the grammar is circular, the generated editor may loop endlessly as it tries to update attribute values in the syntax tree. A circularity test is performed if the sgen flag −K is used.

2.4. Function Declarations

A function is a rule for determining a new term given some number of argument terms. Three kinds of functions may be used in editor specifications: functions written in SSL, predefined library routines, and foreign functions (procedures written in C that can be called from within SSL).

The form of a *function declaration* is

---

phylum$_0$ *function-name* (
       phylum$_1$ *parameter-name*$_1$,
       phylum$_2$ *parameter-name*$_2$,
       . . . ,
       phylum$_k$ *parameter-name*$_k$
) { *expression* } ;

It declares *function-name* to be a k-ary function with result phylum *phylum*$_0$, and has, for each i, $1 \le i \le k$, a parameter named *parameter-name*$_i$ of type *phylum*$_i$. The body of the function, *expression*, is an expression over *parameter-name*$_1$, . . . , *parameter-name*$_k$ that must evaluate to a term in the result phylum *phylum*$_0$.

The phyla used to declare parameter types and the return type of a function must be declared earlier in the specification. Function declarations are global — they cannot be defined inside one another nor can they be defined within the scope of productions. The body of a function cannot access attribute values unless those attributes have been passed to the function as arguments. Functions are not first-class objects, *i.e.* they cannot be the value of a parameter or an attribute. Functions can be recursive. Tail recursive calls are implemented iteratively.

The parameter and result types of functions can be parametric. See Section 2.11, "Quantified Declarations," for further details.

Example 2.4(a). The following declaration defines lookup, a recursive function of two arguments, id and env. Lookup searches env for a binding associated with identifier id and returns the first such binding found. If env contains no binding for id, lookup returns Binding("?",0). The body of the function is explained in Example 2.5.6(a).

```
/* 121 */      BINDING lookup(ID id, ENV env) {
/* 122 */          with (env) (
/* 123 */              NullEnv: Binding("?", 0),
/* 124 */              EnvConcat(b, e):
/* 125 */                  with (b) (Binding(s, *): ( id==s ? b : lookup(id, e)))
/* 126 */          )
/* 127 */      };
```

2.5. Expressions

Expressions are formulae denoting unattributed terms. They occur in attribute equations of productions, in function declarations, in transformation declarations, and, in a limited way, in unparsing declarations.

2.5.1. Variables

A *variable* is a name bound to a *value*. The different lexical contexts of expressions give rise to the distinct sorts of variables itemized below.

Phylum occurrences of productions

The *phylum-name* and the $phylum_i$ of a production

$phylum\text{-}name$: $operator\text{-}name$ ($phylum_1 \ phylum_2 \ \cdots \ phylum_k$) ;

are known as the *phylum occurrences* of the production. Within the attribute equations of a production, each phylum occurrence is a variable whose value is the term derived from that occurrence in the particular instance of that production. The type of such a variable is the given phylum. Let X be one of the phyla occurring in the given production. If phylum X occurs only once in the production, then the name X is sufficient to identify that occurrence. If phylum X occurs more than once, then the names $X\$1$, $X\$2$, *etc.* identify the different occurrences of X in the production: $X\$1$ denotes the first (leftmost) occurrence of X, $X\$2$ denotes the second occurrence of X, *etc.* The abbreviation $\$\$$ is a synonym for *phylum-name*.

Phylum occurrences of entry declarations

As described in Section 2.7.2, entry declarations are used to establish a linkage between a nonterminal in an abstract syntax tree being edited and the root non-terminal of the parse tree for some input text. The two phyla *abstract-syntax-phylum* and *concrete-syntax-phylum* in an entry declaration of the form

abstract-syntax-phylum
    ~ *concrete-syntax-phylum* . *attribute-name* { *equations* } ;

are the entry declaration's *phylum occurrences*. Within the attribute equations of an entry declaration, *abstract-syntax-phylum* is a variable denoting the selected subterm or sublist of the edited buffer; *concrete-syntax-phylum* is a variable denoting the parse tree of the parsed input text. The type of such a variable is the given phylum. If these phyla are distinct, their names are sufficient to identify the given occurrences. If both occurrences are of the same phylum X, then the names $X\$1$ and $X\$2$ are used to distinguish between them. The abbreviation $\$\$$ is a synonym for *abstract-syntax-phylum*.

Attributes of phylum occurrences in productions and entry declarations

The synthesized and inherited attributes of the phylum occurrences within a production or entry declaration are variables. The type of such a variable is the type of the attribute, as specified in its declaration. Let X (respectively $X\$i$ or $\$\$$) denote a phylum occurrence in a given production or entry declaration, as described above. Let a be one of the previously declared attributes of that phylum. Then $X.a$ (respectively $X\$i.a$ or $\$\$.a$) denotes that attribute. The value of the attribute is determined by its defining equation.

Local attributes of productions and entry declarations

Within the attribute equations of a production or entry declaration, each local attribute of the production or entry declaration is a variable whose value is determined by its corresponding attribute equation. The type of such a variable is the type of the attribute, as specified in its declaration. A local attribute's name denotes the attribute; the attribute's declaration must precede any use of its name in an attribute equation.

Upward remote attribute sets

Within the attribute equations of a production p, it is possible to refer to certain attributes of other productions. In particular, the notation

$$\{identifier_1.attribute\text{-}name_1, \ldots, identifier_n.attribute\text{-}name_n\}$$

defines a variable known as an *upward remote attribute set*, which refers to attributes in productions that necessarily occur above any instance of production p in a term. By "above," we mean "between any instance of p and the root of the term." Each *identifier$_i$* is either a phylum name or an operator name. If *identifier$_i$* is a phylum name, then *attribute-name$_i$* must be the name of a synthesized or inherited attribute of that phylum; if *identifier$_i$* is an operator name, then *attribute-name$_i$* must be the name of a local attribute of a production with that operator. All such attributes must have the same type, which is also the type of the upward remote attribute set itself.

The value of an upward remote attribute set in a given instance of production p is the value of the *identifier$_i$.attribute-name$_i$* that occurs first on the path from the given production instance to the root of the term in which it occurs, not including the given production instance or its left-hand-side phylum. If an upward remote attribute set refers to a production's local attribute as well as to an attribute of the production's left-hand-side phylum, the value of the upward remote attribute set is that of the local attribute.

For an upward remote attribute set occurring in production p to be well-formed, at least one of the *identifier$_i$.attribute-name$_i$* must be guaranteed to occur above p in every conceivable context in which p is a subterm. Furthermore, each *identifier$_i$* must be distinct.

Note that upward remote attribute sets in the attribute equations of the concrete input syntax and entry declarations can refer to attributes in the abstract syntax. See Section 2.7.2, "Entry declarations," for a further discussion of this point.

Parameters of functions

Each parameter of a function is a variable that denotes the value of the corresponding argument passed to the function. The type of such a variable is the one specified for the parameter in the function declaration.

Pattern variables

Patterns, as described in Section 2.5.6, "Conditional and binding expressions," contain pattern variables. Patterns occur in with-expressions, let-expressions, and transformations. As a result of pattern matching, each pattern variable is bound to some term. Each pattern variable p has a scope within which p is a variable that denotes the term to which it has been bound. The type of a pattern variable p is determined by the context in which it first occurs in a pattern. This context is either the i-th argument of some operator g, in which case the type of p is the phylum specified for the i-th parameter of g, or it is an entire pattern, in which case the type of p is the type of the expression against which p is being matched.

Attributes of pattern variables

If a pattern is matched against an attributed term, then the values bound to the pattern's pattern variables are attributed. If pattern variable p is bound to an attributed term of a phylum with inherited or synthesized attribute a, then $p.a$ is a variable that denotes the corresponding attribute instance of that term. The type of an attribute is the type specified in its declaration. In the current implementation, this sort of variable is only permitted in transformations, as described in Section 2.8.

2.5.2. Application of functions, operators, and maps

The application of a k-ary function, operator, or map to k arguments of the appropriate phyla, denoted in prefix notation, is an expression.

Function applications

A function application has the form

$$\boxed{\textit{function-name} \ (\ \textit{expression}_1, \ \ldots \ , \textit{expression}_k \ )}$$

Assume that *function-name* has been declared by

phylum$_0$ *function-name* (

    phylum$_1$ *parameter-name*$_1$,

    . . . ,

    phylum$_k$ *parameter-name*$_k$

) { *expression* } ;

and further assume that arguments *expression*$_1$, . . . , *expression*$_k$ have values $v_1, \ldots, v_k$, respectively. Then the value of the function application is the value of *expression* evaluated in an environment in which parameters *parameter-name*$_1$, . . . , *parameter-name*$_k$ are bound to $v_1, \ldots, v_k$, respectively. The types of *expression*$_1$, . . . , *expression*$_k$ must be *phylum*$_1$, . . . , *phylum*$_k$, respectively. The type of the application is *phylum*$_0$. If *function-name* is nullary, an empty pair of parentheses is still required to indicate function application.

Example 2.5.2(a). The right-hand side of the following attribute equation (from Appendix A) is a function application:

/* 143 */   b = lookup(ID, exp.env);

The equation defines the value of local attribute b in production exp:Use(ID). Attribute b is thereby defined to be the result of applying function lookup to subterm ID (the identifier that occurs at exp) and exp.env (the inherited environment attribute in the given context). Attribute b is assigned the value bound to the identifier in the given scope.

Operator applications

An operator application has the form

> *operator-name* (*expression*$_1$, . . . , *expression*$_k$)

Assume the operator has been declared by

phylum-name : *operator-name* (*phylum*$_1$ *phylum*$_2$ $\cdots$ *phylum*$_k$) ;

and further assume that arguments *expression*$_1$, . . . , *expression*$_k$ have values $v_1, \ldots, v_k$, respectively. Then the value of the operator application is the term *operator-name*($v_1, \ldots, v_k$). The types of *expression*$_1$, . . . , *expression*$_k$ must be *phylum*$_1$, . . . , *phylum*$_k$, respectively. The type of the application is *phylum-name*. If *operator-name* is nullary, the empty parenthesis pair can be omitted;

i.e., a nullary operator name, by itself, signifies the term constructed by that operator.

Although the completing term and the placeholder term of a phylum, as defined in Section 2.2, can be explicitly written using operator applications, the following syntax is provided for abbreviation:

Constant	Meaning
[*phylum*]	completing term
<*phylum*>	placeholder term

Example 2.5.2(b). In the SSL specification of the desk calculator found in Appendix A, the constant <exp> denotes Null(), the placeholder term of phylum exp. For example, in the transformation declaration

/* 40 */   transform exp on "+" <exp> : Sum (<exp>, <exp>);

the pattern <exp> denotes the term Null() and the replacement expression Sum(<exp>,<exp>) denotes the term Sum(Null(),Null()). (The fact that the desk calculator also displays Null() as <exp> is essentially a coincidence, a consequence of the fact that the unparsing scheme on line 31 of the specification declares the display representation of Null() to be "<exp>".)

Map applications

A map application has the form

map-valued-expression (*expression*$_1$)

Suppose the value of the *map-valued-expression* is m, a map contained in phylum MAP[*phylum*$_1$,*phylum*$_2$], and further assume that argument *expression*$_1$ has value v_1. Then the the value of the map application is the image of v_1 under mapping m, as defined in Section 2.5.3 under MAP[α,β]. The type of *expression*$_1$ must be *phylum*$_1$. The type of the application is *phylum*$_2$.

Example 2.5.2(c). The right-hand side of the following attribute equation (from Appendix A) is an application of a map:

/* 145A */   exp.v = exp.env(ID);

The equation defines the value of synthesized attribute exp.v in production exp:Use(ID). Attribute v is defined to be the result of applying map exp.env (the inherited environment attribute in the given context) to subterm ID (the identifier used in the expression). Thereby, attribute exp.v is assigned the value bound to the identifier in the given scope.

2.5.3. Operations on primitive phyla

A collection of operations on primitive values is built into SSL. Operations for which special syntax is provided are summarized in Figure 2.2; library functions are summarized in Figure 2.3; relational operations are described in Section 2.5.5.

BOOL

The standard logical operations are provided. "Short-circuit," left-to-right evaluation is used; *i.e.* $p \| q$ is true if p evaluates to true and $p \&\& q$ is false if p evaluates to false, regardless of whether evaluation of q is well-defined. Predicate in is described together with the map operations, below.

INT

The standard arithmetic operations on signed integers are provided. The precision of the integers is machine specific. Division by zero will cause a running editor to crash. Overflow is ignored, *i.e.* +, −, and * are total but, if the result is out of range, it is arbitrary. The modulus operation yields the remainder from the division of the left operand by the right operand.

REAL

The standard arithmetic operations on single-precision floating-point numbers are provided. The precision of the floating-point numbers is machine specific. Underflow is ignored. Overflow and division by zero will cause a running editor to crash. If one operand is REAL and the other is INT, the expression is type incorrect, since there is no implicit type conversion.

Result	Syntax	Operation
BOOL	b_1 && b_2	logical conjunction of b_1 and b_2
	$b_1 \,\|\|\, b_2$	logical disjunction of b_1 and b_2
	$!\,b$	logical negation of b
	e in m	e is in the domain of map m
INT	$i_1 \,^*\, i_2$	product of i_1 and i_2
	$i_1 \,/\, i_2$	quotient of i_1 and i_2
	$i_1 + i_2$	sum of i_1 and i_2
	$i_1 - i_2$	difference of i_1 and i_2
	$i_1 \,\%\, i_2$	i_1 mod i_2
	$i_1 \,\&\, i_2$	bitwise-and of i_1 and i_2
	$i_1 \,\hat{}\, i_2$	bitwise-exclusive-or of i_1 and i_2
	$i_1 \,\|\, i_2$	bitwise-inclusive-or of i_1 and i_2
	$-i$	negation of i
	$\sim i$	bitwise-complement of i
REAL	$r_1 \,^*\, r_2$	product of r_1 and r_2
	$r_1 \,/\, r_2$	quotient of r_1 and r_2
	$r_1 + r_2$	sum of r_1 and r_2
	$r_1 - r_2$	difference of r_1 and r_2
	$-r$	negation of r
CHAR	$s[i]$	i-th character of string s
STR	$s_1 \,\#\, s_2$	concatenation of s_1 and s_2
	$s[i_1:i_2]$	substring of s between i_1 and i_2
	$s[i:]$	substring of s from i to end
PTR	&e	reference to value e
ATTR	&&a	reference to attribute a
MAP[α,β]	$[\alpha|->e]$	empty map from α with default e
	$[\alpha|->e_1,e_2]$	map from α defined by list e_2 with default e_1
	$m[e_1|->e_2]$	map m updated so image of e_1 is e_2
	$m_1[m_2]$	map m_1 updated with map m_2
unknown	$^*p$	dereference a PTR p

Figure 2.2. Operations on the primitive phyla. (In this table, b's are BOOL parameters, i's are INT parameters, r's are REAL parameters, s's are STR parameters, p's are PTR parameters, m's are MAP parameters, e's are parameters of arbitrary type, and α and β are phyla.)

Result	Function(parameters)	Operation
INT	CHARtoINT(CHAR c)	ASCII code for c
	Min(INT i_1, INT i_2)	minimum of i_1 and i_2
	Max(INT i_1, INT i_2)	maximum of i_1 and i_2
	REALtoINT(REAL r)	r truncated to an integer
	STRindex(STR s, CHAR c)	position of leftmost c in s
	STRlen(STR s)	length of s
	STRtoINT(STR s)	s converted to an integer
REAL	INTtoREAL(INT i)	i converted to a real
	STRtoREAL(STR s)	s converted to a real
CHAR	INTtoCHAR(INT i)	character with ASCII code i
STR	gensym(STR s, PTR p)	s # (string representation of p)
	INTtoSTR(INT i)	string representation of i
	repeatCHAR(CHAR c, INT n)	n repetitions of c
	REALtoSTR(REAL r)	string representation of r
	STRtolower(STR s)	s, with all letters lower case
	STRtoupper(STR s)	s, with all letters upper case
TABLE[α]	MakeTable(α l, INT j)	convert list of items l to table
α	Lookup(TABLE[α] h, STR s)	find items in table h with key s
α	UnmakeTable(TABLE[α] h)	convert table h to list of items

Figure 2.3. Library functions on the primitive phyla. (In this table, i's are INT parameters, r's are REAL parameters, c's are CHAR parameters, s's are STR parameters, p's are PTR parameters, h's are TABLE parameters, and α is a phylum.)

CHAR

Conversion between characters and their integer ASCII code is provided. Although any eight-bit character is permitted, the display of non-printing characters is undefined.

STR

Operations on strings of 0 or more characters are provided. The elements of a string s are indexed 1 through STRlen(s). Mixfix notation is provided for selecting the i-th character, $s[i]$, the i-th through j-th characters, $s[i:j]$, and the i-th through the last character of a string, $s[i:]$. Substring selection beyond the boundaries of a string is permitted and results in a substring that consists of just those characters of s lying within the indexed region. If $i < 1$ or $i >$ STRlen(s) then $s[i]$ is undefined.

PTR

If *e* is an expression, then &*e* is a PTR-valued expression known as a *reference* to the value of *e*. Two reference values are equal if and only if they are references to the same instance of a term.

The expression &$$ in a production's attribute equation produces a value unique to each instance of the production. This is particularly useful in conjunction with the built-in function gensym(), which creates a STR by concatenating the first argument (a STR) onto the STR representation of the second argument (a PTR).

References are also useful if one wishes to treat values as being equal only when they are identically equal (as with Lisp's *eq* predicate). This effect is achieved by expressing computations with references to values rather than with a value directly; whenever a PTR's actual value is needed, the PTR is dereferenced.

Considerable care should be exercised in using references. The SSL typechecker will not provide a warning should a dereferenced PTR be used in an incorrect context. Furthermore, since memory management uses reference counting, circular values constructed with pointers will never be reclaimed.

ATTR

If *a* is an attribute variable, then &&*a* is an ATTR-valued expression known as an *attribute reference*. Two attribute references are equal if and only if they are references to the same attribute instance.

Attribute references are of limited utility in that the dereferencing operation is not provided, except through nonstandard, foreign functions. (See Chapter 5, "Interface to C.")

TABLE[α]

There is a limited facility for using hash tables that are indexed by STR-valued keys. The items contained in a hash table are either strings or tuples. If the elements of a table are tuples, then one particular element of each tuple, say the *i*-th, is designated as the key and must be of type STR. Operations MakeTable and UnmakeTable convert back and forth between lists of items and hash tables containing those items. Operation Lookup returns a list of all items with a given key.

Let *phylum*$_1$ be a list phylum consisting of lists of *phylum*$_2$ values, where *phylum*$_2$ is the phylum of items to be stored in a hash table. Phylum *phylum*$_1$ must be declared as a list phylum, as described in Section 2.2.3. Let l be a value of *phylum* $_1$. Let i be an integer specifying the location, within *phylum* $_2$ values, of the string-valued keys. If *phylum* $_2$ is STR, i must be 0 and the key is the STR itself. If *phylum* $_2$ is a user-defined phylum, the i-th parameter of every alternative of *phylum* $_2$ must be of type STR and the i-th argument of an item must be its key. Then the three functions dealing with hash tables are defined, as follows:

1) *MakeTable.* Let l be a value of *phylum* $_1$ and i be an INT, as described above. Then MakeTable(l,i) creates a hash table of type TABLE[*phylum* $_1$], containing the same items as are contained in list l, indexed by element i.

2) *Lookup.* Let h be a hash table of type TABLE[*phylum* $_1$] and let s be a string. Then Lookup(h,s) returns a value of type *phylum* $_1$ that lists, in arbitrary order, all *phylum* $_2$ items in h having key s. Lookup(h,s) lists duplicate values with key s as many times as they occur in h.

3) *UnmakeTable.* Let h be a hash table of type TABLE[*phylum* $_1$]. Then UnmakeTable(h) returns a value of type *phylum* $_1$ that lists, in arbitrary order, all items contained in h. UnmakeTable(h) lists duplicate values as many times as they occur in h.

MAP[α,β]

An instance of parameterized phylum MAP[α,β] contains mappings from phylum α to phylum β. Each such map m is total; *i.e.* for every term t in α, the image of t under m, $m(t)$, is defined. Each map has an associated *default value*, some term in β. Each map is finite in the sense that all but a finite number of terms in α map to the default value. Four map-valued operations are provided:

1) *Empty map.* Suppose e, an expression of type *phylum* $_2$, has value v. Then the expression [*phylum* $_1$|->e] creates an empty map of type MAP[*phylum* $_1$,*phylum* $_2$] with default value v. Let t be a term of *phylum* $_1$. Then

   [*phylum* $_1$|->e](t) has value v, and
   t in [*phylum* $_1$|->e] evaluates to false.

2) *Initialized map.* Suppose e_1, an expression of type *phylum* $_2$, has value v. Further suppose the value of e_2, an expression of some list phylum, lists the values $op(d_1,r_1), \ldots, op(d_n,r_n)$, for some operator op, each d_i in *phylum* $_1$, and each r_i in *phylum* $_2$. Then the expression [*phylum* $_1$|->e_1,e_2] creates a map of type MAP[*phylum* $_1$,*phylum* $_2$], with default value v, mapping

$d_1, \ldots, d_n$ to $r_1, \ldots, r_n$, respectively. If $d_i == d_j$, for some $i \leq j$, then d_i is mapped to r_j.

3) *Single-point update.* Let m be a map of type MAP[$phylum_1, phylum_2$]. Suppose e_1, an expression of type $phylum_1$, has value v_1, and e_2, an expression of type $phylum_2$, has value v_2. Then the expression $m[e_1|->e_2]$ creates a map that is identical to m everywhere except, possibly, at the one point v_1. Let t be a term of $phylum_1$. Then

$m[e_1|->e_2](t)$ has value v_2, if t is equal to v_1,
$m[e_1|->e_2](t)$ has value $m(t)$, if t is not equal to v_1, and
t in $m[e_1|->e_2]$ is equivalent to $(t == v_1) || (t$ in $m)$.

4) *Multiple-point update.* Suppose m_1 and m_2 are maps of type MAP[$phylum_1, phylum_2$]. Then the expression $m_1[m_2]$ creates a map m' of type MAP[$phylum_1, phylum_2$], defined as follows. Let t be a term of $phylum_1$. Then

$m'(t)$ is equal to $m_2(t)$, if t in m_2,
$m'(t)$ is equal to $m_1(t)$, if it is not the case that t in m_2, and
t in m' is equivalent to $(t$ in $m_1) || (t$ in $m_2)$.

Example 2.5.3(a). The following excerpt from the alternative version of the desk calculator (of Appendix A) uses maps to implement environments of name-value bindings. On line 134A, the environment at the root of an expression is defined to be an empty map with default value 0; consequently, any undefined identifier is mapped to 0. On line 137A, the environment in which the let body is to be evaluated is defined to contain the additional name-value binding specified by the let construct. On line 145A, the binding of an identifier is retrieved by applying the environment attribute to the given identifier.

```
/* 130A */      exp { inherited MAP[ID,INT] env; };
/* 134A */      calc: CalcPair { exp.env = [ID |-> 0]; } ;
/* 135A */      exp: Let {
/* 136A */          exp$2.env = exp$1.env;
/* 137A */          exp$3.env = exp$1.env [symb.id |-> exp$2.v];
/* 138A */          exp$1.v = exp$3.v;
/* 139A */          }
/* 140A */       | Use {
/* 144A */          error = (ID in exp.env) ? "<—UNDEFINED" : "";
/* 145A */          exp.v = exp.env(ID);
/* 146A */          } ;
```

2.5.4. List operations

Special syntax is provided for the operations on list phyla of *concatenation*, which attaches a single element to the head of a list, and *append*, which joins two lists:

Operations on list phyla		
Notation	Operation	Usage
::	concatenation	binary infix
@	append	binary infix

If the left operand of a concatenation is an expression of type q, then the right operand must be an expression of type "list of q." The left and right operands of append must be expressions whose type is the same list phylum.

    The concatenate and append operations are provided merely to abbreviate expressions that construct lists; a list phylum's two operators can still be used in the standard fashion to denote the construction of lists. (See Section 2.5.2, "Application of functions, operators, and maps.")

    No special notation is currently provided for specifying lists and sublists in patterns. The nullary and binary operators of a list phylum can be used explicitly in patterns. (See Section 2.5.6, "Conditional and binding expressions.")

2.5.5. Relational operations

Six **BOOL**-valued relational operations, denoted by binary infix operators, are predefined:

Result	Syntax	Operation
BOOL	$e_1 < e_2$	e_1 less than e_2
	$e_1 <= e_2$	e_1 less than or equal to e_2
	$e_1 > e_2$	e_1 greater than e_2
	$e_1 >= e_2$	e_1 greater than or equal to e_2
	$e_1 == e_2$	e_1 equal to e_2
	$e_1 != e_2$	e_1 not equal to e_2

The two arguments of a relational expression must be expressions of the same type. The ordering between values of the same primitive phylum is defined as follows:

Phylum	Ordering
BOOL	false < true
INT	Arithmetic order
REAL	Arithmetic order
CHAR	ASCII order
STR	Lexicographic order
PTR	Arbitrary
ATTR	Arbitrary
TABLE[α]	Arbitrary
MAP[α,β]	Lexicographic order

The notion of order for phyla **PTR**, **ATTR**, and **TABLE** is somewhat arbitrary and should not be relied on.

Let t_1 and t_2 be **TABLE** values MakeTable(l_1,i_1) and MakeTable(l_2,i_2), respectively. Then t_1 and t_2 are equal if and only if i_1 == i_2 and UnmakeTable(t_1) == UnmakeTable(t_2).

Two maps are equal if and only if they have equal default values and identical domain-range pairs. Ordering between maps is lexicographic, depending first on the default values, and then on listings of the domain-range pairs of the maps ordered by domain value. For example,

[STR|–>0] < [STR|–>1]
[STR|–>0] < [STR|–>0]["a"|–>0]
[STR|–>0]["a"|–>0] < [STR|–>0]["a"|–>1]
[STR|–>0]["a"|–>1] < [STR|–>0]["b"|–>0]
[STR|–>0]["b"|–>0]["a"|–>999] < [STR|–>0]["b"|–>0]

Two terms of a user-defined phylum are equal if and only if they are structurally isomorphic. The ordering between terms of a user-defined phylum is lexicographic. User-defined operators are ordered arbitrarily. The ordering between two terms $f(t_1, \ldots, t_k)$ and $f'(t'_1, \ldots, t'_{k'})$ depends first on the ordering between f and f' and thereafter on the lexicographic ordering between the lists of subterms $t_1, \ldots, t_k$ and $t'_1, \ldots, t'_{k'}$. For example, assume f, g, and h are operators, with f < g. Then

f(1) < g(1)
h(1,f(1)) < h(2,f(1))
h(1,f(1)) < h(1,g(1))

2.5.6. Conditional and binding expressions

Conditional and binding expressions permit the value of an expression to depend on the value of a constituent subexpression. Three forms are allowed: *with-expressions*, *conditional-expressions*, and *let-expressions*.

With-expressions

A *with-expression* is a multi-branch conditional expression that permits discrimination based on the structure of the value of a given expression. The syntax of a with-expression is

with (*expression*$_0$) (
pattern$_1$: *expression*$_1$,
pattern$_2$: *expression*$_2$,
. . .
pattern$_n$: *expression*$_n$
)

The value of *expression*$_0$ is called the *matched value*. The value of the with-expression is the value of the *expression*$_i$ corresponding to the first *pattern*$_i$ that *matches* the value of *expression*$_0$. Each *pattern*$_i$ may contain *pattern variables*, which, if the match succeeds, are bound to constituents of the matched value. The value of *expression*$_i$ is then computed in terms of those bindings. The types of all *expression*$_i$ must be the same phylum p; the type of the entire with-expression is that phylum p.

The patterns of a given with-expression must be exhaustive, *i.e.* it must be possible for the compiler to determine statically that for every evaluation of the given with-expression, one of the patterns will match. This will always be the case if one of the patterns is * or default.

Patterns are defined inductively, as follows:

1) Constants of primitive phyla are patterns.
2) [*phylum*] and <*phylum*> are patterns, for every *phylum*.
3) Pattern variables are patterns. A pattern variable is an identifier.
4) Both the symbol * and the keyword default are patterns.
5) A k-ary operator *operator-name* applied to k patterns is a pattern:

> *operator-name* (*pattern*$_1$, . . . , *pattern*$_k$)

If k is 0 and *operator-name* has been declared earlier in the specification, then the parentheses may be omitted. (Warning: an undeclared operator name without parameters will be interpreted as a pattern variable.)

6) A pattern variable, followed by the keyword as, followed by a pattern, is a pattern. As in case 3), a pattern variable is an identifier:

> *pattern-variable-name* as *pattern*

The same pattern variable may occur multiple times in a pattern. The leftmost occurrence of a given pattern variable is its *binding occurrence* and all subsequent occurrences in the same pattern are *bound occurrences*. The type of a pattern variable p is determined by the context of its binding occurrence. This context is either the i-th argument of some operator g, in which case the type of p is the phylum specified for the i-th parameter of g, or it is an entire pattern, in which case the type of p is the type of the expression against which p is being matched.

Let p be a pattern and t be a term. Then p is said to *match* t under the following circumstances:

1) When p is a constant of a primitive phylum and t is that constant.
2) When p is [*phylum*] and t is equal to the *phylum*'s completing term or when p is <*phylum*> and t is equal to the *pylum*'s placeholder term.
3) When p is the binding occurrence of a pattern variable pv, in which case pv is bound to t. When p is a bound occurrence of a pattern variable pv that has been bound to some term t' and $t==t'$.
4) When p is either * or default.
5) When p is $op(p_1, \ldots, p_k)$ and t is $op(t_1, \ldots, t_k)$ and p_i matches t_i for all $i, 1 \le i \le k$.
6) When p is pv as p' and p' matches t and either 6a) this is the defining occurrence of pv or 6b) it is a bound occurrence of pv and pv has been bound to some term t' and $t==t'$.

The lexical scope of a pattern variable bound in some *pattern$_i$* begins at its binding occurrence and extends through the corresponding *expression$_i$*. The scope of pattern variables is block-structured, *i.e.* a given pattern variable may be redeclared in an inner scope.

Example 2.5.6(a). Consider the following definitions of phyla ENV and BINDING from Appendix A:

```
/* 110 */    ENV: NullEnv()
/* 111 */      | EnvConcat( BINDING ENV )
/* 112 */      ;
/* 113 */    BINDING: Binding( ID INT );
```

A value env of phylum ENV is analyzed by the with-expression that is the body of function lookup:

```
/* 121 */    BINDING lookup(ID id, ENV env) {
/* 122 */        with (env) (
/* 123 */          NullEnv: Binding("?", 0),
/* 124 */          EnvConcat(b, e):
/* 125 */              with (b) (Binding(s, *): ( id==s ? b : lookup(id, e)))
/* 126 */          )
/* 127 */      };
```

The two operators NullEnv and EnvConcat exhaust all possible alternatives for ENV, so no default pattern is necessary. If the value of env is NullEnv(), then the pattern NullEnv matches it and the value of the with-expression is Binding("?", 0). Otherwise, the value of env is necessarily a pair and the pattern

EnvConcat(b, e) matches with pattern variables b and e bound to the first and second components, respectively. In this case, the value of the with-expression is the value of the inner with-expression, wherein pattern variables b and e have types BINDING and ENV, respectively.

The same effect can be obtained by combining the two nested with-expressions into one:

```
BINDING lookup(ID id, ENV env) {
  with (env) (
    NullEnv: Binding("?", 0),
    EnvConcat(b as Binding(s, v), e): ( id==s ? b : lookup(id, e)))
  )
};
```

Conditional-expressions

A more traditional form of conditional expression is available in SSL, based not on pattern matching but on the value of a Boolean expression. A *conditional-expression* has the form

$$\boxed{expression_1 \ ? \ expression_2 : expression_3}$$

It is exactly equivalent to the expression

with ($expression_1$) (true : $expression_2$, false : $expression_3$)

Let-expressions

Let-expressions are useful for binding values to names and, when the structure of a value is known in part, for binding local names to its constituents. The simplest form of let-expression is:

$$\boxed{\text{let } pattern_1 = expression_1 \text{ in } (expression)}$$

which is exactly equivalent to

with ($expression_1$)($pattern_1$: $expression$)

When several values are to be matched, a more general form is available:

---

let

    pattern =*expression* and $\cdots$ and *pattern* =*expression* ;

    pattern =*expression* and $\cdots$ and *pattern* =*expression* ;

    . . .

    pattern =*expression* and $\cdots$ and *pattern* =*expression*

in (*expression*$_0$)

Note that the clauses

    pattern = *expression*

are clustered into groups separated by semicolons and that, within a group, clauses are separated by the keyword and. The leftmost occurrence of a pattern variable within a pattern is its binding occurrence and all subsequent occurrences within that pattern are bound occurrences. Although a given pattern variable may be rebound in subsequent and-connected groups, it cannot be bound in more than one pattern within a single and-connected group. For a let-expression to be well-formed, each *pattern* must necessarily match any possible value of the corresponding *expression*. The type of the let-expression is the type of *expression*$_0$. A semicolon before the keyword in is optional.

The value of the general form of let-expression is determined as follows:

Each *pattern* is matched against the value of the corresponding *expression* and its pattern variables bound accordingly. The value of the let-expression is the value of *expression*$_0$ as computed in an environment containing bindings for all pattern variables of all patterns. The *expressions* of each and-connected group of clauses are all evaluated in the same environment, which includes all pattern variables bound in all previous patterns up to but not including those in the given group.

2.5.7. Grouping, sequencing, and precedence

Any expression can be parenthesized for grouping:

(*expression*)

Since the SSL expression language contains no operations with side-effects, the order of evaluation is, in general, irrelevant. However, in order to permit exploitation of side effects caused by the evaluation of foreign functions, the binary infix operation ! is provided. The value of the expression

$$ expression_1 \ ! \ expression_2 $$

is the value of $expression_2$ evaluated after first evaluating $expression_1$. The type of a sequencing expression is the type of $expression_2$.

All unary operations associate to the right and have equal precedence at a level greater than that of any binary operator.

Operator	Association
~, !, −, &, *, &&	right

The precedence of binary infix operations, from highest to lowest, is given in the table shown in Figure 2.4. Operations with equal precedence are shown on the same line.

Operation	Operator	Association
application, update	( ), [ ]	left
string concatenation	#	left
multiply, divide, mod	*, /, %	left
add, subtract	+, −	left
concatenation	::	right
list append	@	left
order	<, <=, >, >=	nonassociating
equality, inequality	==, !=	nonassociating
bitwise and	&	left
bitwise exclusive or	^	left
bitwise or	|	left
logical and	&&	left
logical or	||	left
sequencing	!	left

Figure 2.4. The precedence of binary infix operations, listed from highest to lowest. Operations with equal precedence are shown on the same line.

2.5.8. Conversion of terms to and from strings

Section 2.6 describes declarations that specify how a term can be displayed as text. Section 2.7 describes declarations that specify how text can be parsed and translated to a term. Both of these conversion operations are available within expressions.

Each of the following two forms is an expression:

---

unparse (*expression* , *view-name*)

parse (*expression*$_1$, *phylum* , *expression*$_2$)

Let t be a term and v be a view name. Then unparse(t,v) is an expression of type STR. Its value is the display array $A(S(t,v),w)$, as described in Section 2.6.3, linearized into a string with separate rows of characters separated by newline characters. The width parameter w is the global editor parameter absolute-right-margin. The view parameter can be omitted, in which case it defaults to BASEVIEW.

Let e_1 be an expression of type STR with value s, let p be a phylum, and let e_2 be an expression of type p. Then parse(e_1,p,e_2) is an expression of type p. Its value is the term of type p that would result if s were parsed according to the entry rules for phylum p. Such entry rules are not permitted to contain references to attributes of p. If s contains a syntax error according to these rules, the value of e_2 is returned.

Example 2.5.8(a). Assume we have declared the same phyla as in the desk calculator of Appendix A. Then the value of the expression

unparse(Sum(Const(1),Const(2)))

is the string (1 + 2). Conversely, the value of the expression

parse("(1+2)", exp, Null())

is the term Sum(Const(1),Const(2)).

2.5.9. Attribution expressions

Because attribute types are defined with grammar rules, SSL has a uniform approach to defining structured data: the denotable values in SSL are attributable terms whose attributes are themselves attributable terms, *ad infinitum*. The

expression language permits forcing the attribution of a (previously unattributed) term with *attribution expressions* of the form

expression { equations } . attribute-name

The value of such an expression is computed as follows: (a) the *expression* is
evaluated, yielding some attributable (but as yet unattributed) term T of a phylum for which *attribute-name* is an attribute, (b) the inherited attributes of T are
defined by the given *equations*, (c) the value of T.*attribute-name* is computed
by demand and is returned.

   The use of attribution expressions is not encouraged, since the current implementation is both incomplete and inefficient. At the moment, the equations of
an attribution expression must be empty; however, this limited facility does
allow simulating any desired attribution expression.

   Example 2.5.9(a). We illustrate how such a simulation is carried out by an
example that uses the definitions provided in the desk-calculator specification
given in Appendix A. Suppose we wish to compute the attribution expression

Use("a") { env = Binding("a",4) :: NullEnv; } . v

We define an additional phylum **New** with a single operator **NewOp** consisting
of an **exp** and an **ENV**; an equation specifies that **exp.env** gets the value **ENV**:

New : NewOp(exp ENV) { exp.env = ENV; };

We must also define how **exp.v** is passed to the left-hand side:

New { synthesized INT value; };
New : NewOp { New.value = exp.v; };

The desired attribution expression is then expressed by

NewOp(Use("a"), Binding("a",4) :: NullEnv) { } . value

2.6. View and Unparsing Declarations

The objects manipulated in an editor are attributed terms, each contained in a
named buffer. Buffers are displayed and modified in windows, where each window presents a particular *view* of a buffer. Buffers may be displayed in several

windows simultaneously, with each window offering a different view of the term.

The distinct ways of viewing terms are declared in *view declarations*, which have the form

---
view *view-name*$_1$, . . . , *view-name*$_k$;

View-name$_1$, . . . , *view-name*$_k$ are identifiers. The view **BASEVIEW** is predeclared. If only one manner of viewing terms is desired, no view declarations are required, since windows display buffers in the **BASEVIEW**, by default. The view associated with a window is altered by executing the command **change-view**, as described in Section 3.4. A special sort of view, known as a sparse view, is described in Section 2.6.5.

The display form of a term in a view is determined by a specification's *unparsing declarations*, which determine (a) the two-dimensional textual representation of the term, (b) the selectable components of the term, and (c) the default editing modes of those selectable components.

The basic form of an unparsing declaration is

---
phylum-name : *operator-name* [*view-name unparsing-scheme*] ;
---

which specifies unparsing properties, in the given view, for the production

phylum-name : *operator-name* (*parameters*) ;

The *view-name* component of an unparsing declaration is optional; if omitted, the unparsing scheme is associated with **BASEVIEW**, by default.

Up to two unparsing declarations are permitted for each production-view pair. The lexically first unparsing declaration for a production in a view specifies its *principal unparsing scheme* and the second its *alternate unparsing scheme*. Omitted unparsing declarations are assumed to be

phylum-name : *operator-name* [*view-name* ˆ : ˆ $\cdots$ ˆ] ;

where there are as many ˆ symbols to the right of : as the arity of the named operator.

Each production instance of a term in a buffer has a current *unparsing mode*, either principle or alternate. The principal unparsing scheme is adopted when the production is instantiated. Thereafter, the user may manually toggle between principal and alternate modes using the commands described in Section 3.15, "Alternating Unparsing Schemes." Note that each production instance in a buffer is associated with a single unparsing mode, which determines the unparsing scheme used for displaying that production instance in every view of the buffer.

The form of an *unparsing-scheme* resembles a production — it has left and right sides separated by one of the two symbols : or ::= . Thus, basic unparsing declarations have one of the two forms

---

phylum-name : *operator-name* [*view-name left-side* : *right-side*] ;
phylum-name : *operator-name* [*view-name left-side* ::= *right-side*] ;

The separating symbol (: or ::=) determines the editing mode, as described in Section 2.6.1, below.

Several varieties of factoring support abbreviation of unparsing declarations. First, an unparsing scheme may be declared for several views at once, using the form

---

phylum-name :
    operator-name [*view-name*$_1$, . . . , *view-name*$_k$ *unparsing-scheme*] ;

Second, the unparsing declarations for a given production may appear together with the operator factored to the left, as in

---

phylum-name :
    operator-name
        [*view-name*$_1$, . . . , *view-name*$_k$ *unparsing-scheme*]
        . . .
        [*view-name*$_1$, . . . , *view-name*$_k$ *unparsing-scheme*]
    ;

Third, as with other kinds of declarations, when a number of unparsing declarations are specified for a single phylum, the phylum can be factored to the left; furthermore, an unparsing scheme can be associated with several operators of a phylum in a single declaration:

phylum-name :

    operator-list [*view-name*$_1$, . . . , *view-name*$_k$ *unparsing-scheme*]

    | *operator-list* [*view-name*$_1$, . . . , *view-name*$_k$ *unparsing-scheme*]

    . . .

    | *operator-list* [*view-name*$_1$, . . . , *view-name*$_k$ *unparsing-scheme*]

    ;

2.6.1. Editing modes

Textual re-editing of a term with a given production at its apex is permitted only if an entry declaration for the production's left-hand-side phylum exists. (See Section 2.7, "Concrete Input Syntax.") Assuming such an entry declaration exists, the command **text-capture** makes the textual representation of the term available for modification in an edit buffer, as described in Sections 1, 2.7.1, 3.5, and 3.12.

Because it would be tedious to have to explicitly execute **text-capture** each time text editing is required, it is possible to associate a production with a text-editing mode that causes any textual editing operation such as typing or erasing a character to implicitly execute **text-capture** before the keystroke is processed. On the other hand, because in some contexts inadvertent implicit text-capture can be just as tedious, an alternative editing mode is provided that does not do implicit text-captures. The editing mode of a production is indicated by the separating symbol in the unparsing scheme.

The symbol ::= indicates that textual editing of the production is the norm; in this case, any textual editing operation implicitly converts the production and its constituents into editable text.

The symbol : indicates that the production is ordinarily treated as an immutable structural unit; in this case, the textual representation is editable only after an explicit **text-capture** command. Although a given term may not itself be implicitly textually editable, it may contain subterms that are.

Example 2.6.1(a). In the desk calculator of Appendix A, the unparsing declaration

/* 157 */   exp: Let[@ : "let %t" @ " = " @ " in%n" @ "%b%nni"];

defines unparsing properties of the production

/* 86 */   exp: Let(symb exp exp);

Because the symbol : is used to separate left and right sides of the unparsing scheme, let-expressions are normally treated as immutable structural entities. However, because a concrete input syntax is provided for let-expressions (see lines 150-155 of the specification in Appendix A) they can be entered textually and, with the aid of the **text-capture** command, re-edited textually.

2.6.2. Resting places

We have seen, in Section 2.6, that an unparsing scheme consists of a left-hand side and a right-hand side separated by either the symbol : or the symbol ::=. An unparsing scheme contains *resting-place denoters*, symbols that correspond to the phylum occurrences in the production whose display format is being defined. There are three possible resting-place denoters: .. , @, and ˆ. The left-hand side of an unparsing scheme consists of a single resting-place denoter. Only @ and ˆ are permitted for the left-hand-side phylum occurrence. The right-hand side of an unparsing scheme for a production of arity n contains n resting-place denoters. The left-to-right sequence of resting-place denoters in an unparsing scheme for a given production corresponds to the left-to-right sequence of phylum occurrences in that production. Each of the resting-place denoters for the right-hand side phylum occurrences can be any of the three symbols .. , @, or ˆ.

Resting-place denoters determine the *resting places* of a term, those nodes at which the apex of a selection can rest. Such nodes are said to be *selectable*. The internal structure of a term can be hidden by making some nodes unselectable.

Every node of a term other than the root node and the leaf nodes corresponds to occurrences of a phylum in two productions, one on the right-hand side of a production and the other on the left-hand side. The resting-place properties of such a node are determined by the corresponding resting-place denoters in the unparsing schemes of those two productions. Each root node or leaf node corresponds to just one phylum occurrence. The resting-place property of such a node is determined by the resting-place denoter of that single corresponding phylum occurrence.

The resting-place denoter .. causes suppression of the display of the corresponding subterm. All nodes within a subterm whose display is suppressed are non-resting places.

The resting-place denoter @ indicates a resting place. A node is a resting place if either of the two corresponding phylum occurrences is specified to be a resting place.

The resting-place denoter ˆ indicates a non-resting place. A node is not a resting place if both of the two corresponding phylum occurrences are specified to be non-resting places.

A production's unparsing declaration may be omitted, in which case it is as if the specification had included an unparsing declaration consisting entirely of ˆ symbols for resting-place denoters.

Section 2.6.4, "Unparsing lists," describes special considerations required when specifying resting places in lists.

Example 2.6.2(a). In the desk-calculator specification of Appendix A, the display format of expressions other than let-expressions is defined by the following unparsing declarations:

```
/* 31 */     exp: Null [ @ ::= "<exp>" ]
/* 32 */      | Sum  [ @ ::= "(" @ " + " @ ")" ]
/* 33 */      | Diff   [ @ ::= "(" @ " – " @ ")" ]
/* 34 */      | Prod  [ @ ::= "(" @ " * " @ ")" ]
/* 35 */      | Quot  [ @ ::= "(" @ " / " error @ ")" ]
/* 36 */      | Const [ @ ::= ˆ ]
/* 37 */      ;
```

These rules specify that expressions are to be fully parenthesized, with selectable placeholders, constants, and subexpressions, each of which is editable as text. The subterm INT of Const is not a separate resting place. In production Quot, local attribute error is displayed immediately after the division sign.

2.6.3. Formatting the display representation

Interspersed among the resting-place denoters on the right-hand side of a given production's unparsing scheme are zero or more *unparsing items*. The following unparsing items are supported:

1) quoted STR constants,
2) phylum occurrences of the production,
3) attributes of phylum occurrences of the production,
4) local attributes of the production,
5) conditional unparsing items.

Consideration of conditional unparsing items is deferred until Section 2.6.4, "Unparsing lists."

The display representation of a term t in view v is defined in two stages: first, a *display string* $S(t,v)$, containing both printable characters and formatting characters, is determined from t and v; second, a two-dimensional *display array* $A(S(t,v),w)$ is determined by interpreting $S(t,v)$ given a width w. Informally, the display string is determined by a left-to-right traversal of the term that concatenates unparsing items. The display array consists of the printable characters of the display string broken onto different lines.

The display string

Let t be a term and v be a view. Display string $S(t,v)$ is defined inductively, as follows:

If t is a value of a primitive phylum, then $S(t,v)$ is chosen according to the following table of primitive display formats:

Phylum	Display format
BOOL	false, true
INT	decimal representation of the integer
REAL	decimal exponential representation of the real number
CHAR	the character (unquoted)
STR	the string (unquoted)
PTR	$->node\text{-}address$
ATTR	$<node\text{-}address[attribute\text{-}number]>$
TABLE[α]	TABLE no_elements n key_position k
MAP[α,β]	a list of the domain-range pairs in the map

The display form of unprintable characters is undefined.

If t is not an element of a primitive phylum, then it is of the form $op(t_1,t_2,\ldots,t_n)$ for some operator op and subterms $t_1,\ldots,t_n$. Suppose the currently active unparsing scheme for the given op in the given view v consists of $m \geq n$ resting-place denoters and unparsing items, $e_1, e_2, \ldots, e_m$. Note that n of the e_i are resting-place denoters; interspersed among them are $m-n$ unparsing items. To each e_i there corresponds a value u_i (to be defined below). Display string $S(t,v)$ is defined to be the concatenation of the display strings of these u_i:

$$S(t,v) = S(u_1,v)\, S(u_2,v)\, \cdots\, S(u_m,v)$$

Suppose e_i is the j-th resting-place denoter on the right-hand side of the unparsing scheme. If e_i is either @ or ˆ, then u_i is t_j. If e_i is .. , then u_i is the empty string.

Suppose e_i is an unparsing item.

1) If e_i is a constant of type STR, then u_i is the corresponding string.
2) If e_i is a phylum occurrence denoting the j-th argument of op, then u_i is t_j.
3) If e_i is an attribute occurrence, then the value u_i depends on whether the term t is attributed. If t is attributed, for example, if it is the contents of an editing buffer, then u_i is the value of the corresponding attribute instance. If t is itself an attribute, u_i is the string <attribute value of an attribute>.

Example 2.6.3(a). According to the unparsing declarations:

```
/* 31 */     exp: Null[ @ ::= "<exp>" ]
/* 157 */      | Let[ @ : "let %t" @ " = " @ " in%n" @ "%b%nni" ];
/* 160 */    symb: DefBot[ @ ::= "<name>" ];
```

the term Let(DefBot(),Null(),Null()) is displayed by interpreting the string

let %t<name> = <exp> in%n<exp>%b%nni

The display array

Display array $A(S(t,v),w)$, the two-dimensional textual representation of term t in view v, is created by interpreting each character of display string $S(t,v)$ during a left-to-right scan. Determination of the *line-width parameter* w is described below. In $S(t,v)$, characters preceded by a % are treated as special *formatting commands*. For backwards compatibility with earlier versions of the Synthesizer Generator, the strings \t, \b, \n, and \r are also still considered formatting commands and are synonymous with %t, %b, %n, and %l, respectively. The formatting commands are summarized in Figure 2.5. If %x is not one of the itemized formatting commands, then %x is printed as x. All characters that are not part of formatting commands are displayed as themselves. The result of displaying non-printable characters is not defined.

Two interpretation modes are supported, depending on the value of the SSL compile-time flag format_strings. If format_strings is true, every percent sign that occurs in $S(t,v)$ is interpreted as a formatting command. In particular, this includes percent signs that occur in STR subterms of t and in STR attributes that are displayed. If format_strings is false, percent signs are interpreted as formatting commands only if they arise from the quoted unparsing items of unparsing schemes. See Section 2.10, "Option Declarations," for information on setting flag format_strings. The default value for format_strings is false.

Formatting command	Meaning
%t	move the left-margin one indentation unit to the right
%b	move the left-margin one indentation unit to the left
%n	break the line and return to the current left-margin
%l	return to current left-margin of the same line and overprint
%1	move to column one of the same line and overprint
%T	move right to the next tab stop
%M(c)	move right to column c, where c is a positive integer
%o	optionally, break the line and return to the current left-margin
%c	same as %o, but either all or no %c in a group are taken
%{	beginning of an unparsing group
%}	end of an unparsing group
%[	same as %t%{
%]	same as %}%b
%S(*style-name*:	enter the named style
%S)	revert to the previous style
%%	display a %

Figure 2.5. Formatting commands.

The precise meaning of formatting commands depends, in part, on the values of editor parameters. In particular, the size of indentation units, the position of tab stops, the maximal length of a line, and the regime for handling right margins are adjustable in a running editor. (See the description of the **set-parameters** command in Section 3.1.) The editor parameter **absolute-right-margin** specifies an upper limit for w, the maximal length of lines. In addition, w depends on which of two regimes for the right margin are in effect, *clipping* or *word-wrapping*.

Clipping mode is signified by the editor parameter **word-wrapping** having value **off**. In clipping mode, the maximal line length is independent of window width and the line-width parameter w is the value of **absolute-right-margin**.

In word-wrapping mode, the line-width parameter w is the minimum of **absolute-right-margin** and the sum of the window's width and the distance the window has been scrolled to the right. Thus, assuming that the window has not been scrolled to the right, the display of the term is forced into a column of text no wider than the window. If the window has been scrolled to the right, clipping may occur to the left of the window, but will not occur to the right.

Indentation is often used to indicate the structure of terms. Formatting commands %t and %b adjust the position of the left-margin in support of this practice. Each %t moves the left-margin one indentation unit to the right; each %b, one to the left. The editor parameter indentation specifies the width of each indentation unit. Text following %n is displayed on the next line, beginning at the current left margin. Note that merely changing the left-margin has no immediate visible effect; its effect is evident only after the start of a new line. In word wrapping mode, the left-margin is not permitted further to the right than two-thirds of the window width. Indentation beyond this limit cause the left-margin to wrap back to column one.

Example 2.6.3(b). Continuing the example of the desk-calculator's let-expressions, interpretation of the display string

let %t<name> = <exp> in%n<exp>%b%nni

yields the following two-dimensional array of characters:

let <name> = <exp> in
   <exp>
ni

Example 2.6.3(c). Customarily, the number of %b's in each unparsing declaration balance the number of %t's so that, when a production finishes printing, the indentation level has been restored back to the depth it was at when the printing of the production began. This is illustrated in the display of a term of two nested let-expressions:

Let(DefBot(),Null(),Let(DefBot(),Null(),Null()))

which is displayed as:

let <name> = <exp> in
  let <name> = <exp> in
     <exp>
  ni
ni

Example 2.6.3(d). Attributes are frequently incorporated in the unparsing of a production. Error messages may be defined to be the appropriate text (if an error exists) or the null string (if no error exists). By this device, an error message appears and disappears as the error comes and goes. The technique is illustrated in the desk-calculator's division-by-zero error. The specification

```
exp: Quot{ local STR error;
        error = (exp$3.v == 0) ? "<—DIVISION BY ZERO—>" : "";
        exp$1.v = (exp$3.v == 0) ? exp$2.v : (exp$2.v / exp$3.v);
    }
    [ @ ::= "(" @ " / " error @ ")" ]
    ;
```

has the effect of displaying the sample expression $(8 / (2 - 2))$ as

```
(8 / <—DIVISION BY ZERO—>(2 – 2))
VALUE = 8
```

After modifying the divisor to be $(4 - 2)$, the screen would appear as:

```
(8 / (4 – 2))
VALUE = 4
```

Example 2.6.3(e). Alternate unparsing declarations are illustrated in the desk calculator of Appendix A. The alternate scheme for let-expressions displays the value bound to the name rather than its defining expression:

```
/* 157 */ /* Alternate unparsing declaration for let-expressions */
/* 158 */ exp: Let[ @ : "let %t" @ " = <" .. exp$2.v "> in%n" @ "%b%nni"];
```

The expression displayed with the principal unparsing scheme as

```
let pi = (22 / 7) in
    ((pi * 4) * 4)
ni
VALUE = 48
```

would then be displayed with the above alternate unparsing scheme as:

```
let pi = <3> in
    ((pi * 4) * 4)
ni
VALUE = 48
```

Optional line breaks, indicated by %o, provide a means of specifying preferred places where a term's display string is to be divided into separate lines. If the current line contains no optional line breaks, it will be split just before the first character that would not entirely fit on the line. A hierarchical structure is imposed on the display string by the matched grouping symbols %{ and %}. If optional line breaks are available on a line that needs to be split, an attempt is made to split the line in a manner that divides a minimal number of unparsing

groupings and maximizes the amount of text on the line. A grouping has effect
only if it contains optional line breaks. Note that if indentation is desired only
for text following an optional line break that is taken, one may use the formatting command string %t%o%b.

An alternative form of optional line break, called a *connected break* and indicated by %c, permits specification of a display in which either all text of an
unparsing grouping appears on the same line or all connected line breaks in the
group are taken.

Example 2.6.3(f). Let-expressions can be displayed to take into account the
width of the window by using the following unparsing declaration:

exp: Let[@ : "%{%{let " @ " %o= " @ " in %}%c%[" @ "%] %cni%}"];

The expression displayed in a sufficiently wide window as

let a = (1 + 2) in (a + a) ni

is displayed in a narrower window as

let a = (1 + 2) in
  (a + a)
ni

or in a still narrower window as

let a
= (1 + 2) in
  (a + a)
ni

Four formatting commands offer additional horizontal control on the same
line. Text following %T is displayed beginning at the next tab stop, where the
spacing between tab stops is indicated by the tab-stops editor parameter. Text
following %M(c) is displayed beginning in column c. If more than c columns
of text have already been displayed on the line, %M(c) has no effect. In the
case of variable-width fonts, column c is considered to be the position just
beyond the $(c-1)$-st zero on a line of all zeros. Text following %l is printed
beginning at the left margin; text following %1 beginning at the leftmost position on the line. Inappropriate use of %l and %1 may result in overprinting.

It is sometimes desirable to differentiate different regions of a term's display
by using distinct font sizes and characteristics. For example, one may wish keywords in boldface, placeholders in italics, comments in a different font, and
error messages in yet another font. Each such region corresponds to a distinct

display *style*. Styles are declared in *style declarations*, which have the form

> **style** *style-name*$_1$, ... , *style-name*$_k$;

where *style-name*$_1$, ... , *style-name*$_k$ are each identifiers. The very first style declared is known as the *base style*. If no style is declared anywhere in the specification, default fonts are selected, as described in Appendix D. The name largest is used for other purposes (see below) and should not be used as a style name.

Interpretation of a display string starts in the base style. Formatting command %S(*style-name*: enters the given style and formatting command %S) reverts to the previous style. Thus, at any given point in the interpretation of a display string, a stack of styles *style*$_0$, ... , *style*$_n$ is active, where *style*$_0$ is the base style. Each character in the display array is associated with the stack of styles active at that point in the display string.

The meaning of a style is not bound at editor-generation time. Rather, it is specified in a *style-definition file*, which is read when an editor is executed. Late binding of styles permits local customization based on terminal functionality and personal taste. See Appendix D for details on how style-definition files are named and located.

The format of a style-definition file is as follows.

> **fonts** { *font-name*$_1$, ... , *font-name*$_n$ } ;
> largest : *item* , ... , *item* ;
> *style-name* : *item* , ... , *item* ;
>   ...
> *style-name* : *item* , ... , *item* ;

The first line of a style-definition file lists the names of all fonts used. A *font-name* is the unqualified name of one of the available fonts, *e.g.* a stem without the modifiers that indicate boldface or italic. Both fixed-width and proportional fonts are supported.

The second line of a style-definition file must designate a unique font, possibly with properties such as boldface or italic. The height of this font determines the height of text lines in the object pane.

The remaining lines of a style-definition file characterize styles; there must be one line for each style declared in the SSL specification. An *item* is either a *font-name* or it is a *property*, optionally prefixed by a +, −, or ! character. A *font-name* item signifies that the given font is to be used for the style. If no font is specified for a style, the font of the enclosing style is used. The *properties* are **bold** and *italic*. Properties prefixed by + (or with no prefix) are turned on, those prefixed by − are turned off, and those prefixed by ! are toggled. A property not controlled by a style is unchanged. A given font may not be available with the specified properties, in which case a compromise choice is made.

Example 2.6.3(g). The following is a sample style-definition file:

```
fonts { timrom12, helv12 } ;
largest : timrom12, +bold ;
Normal : timrom12 ;
Keyword : +bold ;
Placeholder : +italic ;
Comment : helv12 ;
```

Example 2.6.3(h). The following sample unparsing declarations illustrate how keywords and placeholders can be displayed in distinct styles.

```
style Normal, Keyword, Placeholder;
exp: Null[ @ ::= "%S(Placeholder:<exp>%S)" ]
  | Let[ @ :
      "%S(Keyword:let%S) %t" @ " = " @ " %S(Keyword:in%S)%n"
        @ "%b%n"
      "%S(Keyword:ni%S)"
    ]
  ;
```

When used in conjunction with the style-definition file of Example 2.6.3(g), placeholders are printed in italics and keywords in boldface. For example,

let *<name>* = *<exp>* **in**
  <exp>
ni

2.6.4. Unparsing lists

It is recommended that certain conventions be followed in writing unparsing schemes for list phyla. One question concerning the unparsing of lists is how to obtain unparsing text that separates rather than terminates list items. Recall that a phylum declared to be a list has two productions, one nullary and the other binary and right-recursive. For example, consider the declaration

```
list id_list;
id_list: IdListNil()
  | IdListCons( identifier id_list)
  ;
```

where phylum identifier is defined as

```
identifier: IdPlaceholder()
  | Id( STR )
  ;
```

Suppose that in the unparsing of an id_list identifiers are to be separated with commas. The unparsing declaration:

```
id_list: IdListCons[ @ ::= @ "," @ ]
```

would be incorrect, since it would also display a comma after the last identifier. To understand this, recall that an id_list is terminated by production IdListNil. For example, the term containing identifiers "a", "b", and "c" is

```
IdListCons(Id("a"),IdListCons(Id("b"),IdListCons(Id("c"),IdListNil())))
```

A solution is provided by using a *conditional unparsing item*, a list of unparsing items enclosed in square brackets. A conditional unparsing item may only appear in the binary production of a list phylum; it is only displayed when the second subterm of that production is also the binary production of the list phylum. Thus, the correct way to obtain a comma-separated list is

```
id_list: IdListCons[ @ ::= @ [","] @ ]
```

Characters displayed within a conditional unparsing item have an additional useful property: selecting one with the mouse or other locating device causes the selection to move to a placeholder term grafted between the two adjacent list items.

A second question concerning lists involves eliminating the distinction between list items and sublists that contain only one item. In a running editor, the selection is either an entire subterm or a sublist. Sublists represent interior structures that are not actually complete terms. For example, the sublist consisting of just the identifiers a and b would be the term:

```
IdListCons(Id("a"),IdListCons(Id("b"),*))
```

where * denotes the tail of the list that has been excluded from the sublist. The singleton sublist containing just the identifier b would be the term:

IdListCons(Id("b"),*)

which is a different term from the term Id("b").

The following practice is recommended: make individual items in a list non-resting places and make nodes of the list phylum resting places. In the example, this would be accomplished by the following unparsing declarations:

id_list: IdListNil[ˆ :]
   | IdListCons[@ ::= ˆ [","] @]
   ;
identifier: IdPlaceholder[ˆ ::= "<identifier>"]
   | Id[ˆ ::= ˆ]
   ;

A special property of transformations further supports this practice; when the selection is a singleton list item, all transformations that would have been enabled had the selection been just that item are also enabled. (See Section 2.8, "Transformation Declarations," for further details.)

2.6.5. Sparse views

A *sparse view* is a special kind of view. Sparse views are declared in *sparse-view declarations*, which have the form

sparse view *view-name*$_1$, . . . , *view-name*$_k$;

In a normal (dense) view, the display representation is determined from the entire term. In particular, the display of term t in view v with width w is the array of characters $A(S(t,v),w)$, as described in Section 2.6.3. In contrast, in a sparse view, the display representation is defined with respect to a subset of the term's nodes, referred to as *nontrivial nodes*. Let N be a set of nontrivial nodes of term t (determined in a manner to be discussed in the next paragraph). Then the display representation of term t with nontrivial nodes N in sparse view v with width w is the display array $A(S(projection(t,N),v),w)$. The tree denoted by $projection(t,N)$ consists of the nodes N of t, closed under the least-common-ancestor relation. Each node in $projection(t,N)$ has an edge to its nearest ancestor node. Although operators label the nodes of *projection* (t, N), the arity and argument types of the operators are not respected in the projection. Therefore, strictly speaking, *projection* (t, N) is not a well-formed term. If N is empty, *projection* (t, N) is the null tree.

The nontrivial nodes of a term in a given sparse view are determined as follows: for each sparse view, each production has an optional *view predicate*, a BOOL-valued expression defined in terms of the attributes of the production. The nontrivial nodes of a term are precisely the nodes whose view predicates have the value true. A *view-predicate declaration* has the form

---

in *view-name*$_1$, . . . , *view-name*$_k$ on *expression* ;

View predicates are defined on a production-by-production basis together with the local attributes and the attribute equations of the production. For example,

---

phylum-name : *operator-name* {

   . . .

   in *view-name*$_1$, . . . , *view-name*$_k$ on *expression* ;

   . . .

  } ;

---

specifies that, in each of *view-name*$_1$, . . . , *view-name*$_k$, nodes labeled with *operator-name* are nontrivial if and only if the given *expression* has the value true.

Attribute values that are displayed in the unparsing of a term in a sparse view are always displayed in their entirety. A window displaying a buffer in a sparse view is read only.

Example 2.6.5(a). A local editing change can introduce numerous remote effects, which are likely to go unnoticed if their position is outside the window. Sparse views are particularly useful for making such effects apparent. Consider adding the following declarations to the desk calculator of Appendix A:

```
sparse view errorview;
exp: Quot [ errorview @ : .. error .. ]
        { in errorview on error != ""; }
    |  Use [ errorview @ : .. error ]
        { in errorview on error != ""; }
    ;
```

According to these declarations, an errorview displays just nodes with error messages that are not the empty string.

For example, consider the term displayed in a BASEVIEW as

let x = 4 in (((1 / x) * (2 / x)) + (3 / x))

An errorview of this term is empty, since all error attributes are null.

Now suppose that the 4 is changed to 0, resulting in three attempts to divide by zero. Then each Quot node of the resulting term

```
Let(
  Def("x"),
  Const(0),
  Sum(
    Prod( Quot(Const(1),Use(x)), Quot(Const(2),Use(x)) ),
    Quot(Const(3),Use(x))
    )
  )
```

is nontrivial, because its error attribute is not the null string. The projection with respect to these nontrivial nodes is

Sum(Prod(Quot( ),Quot( )),Quot( ))

which would be displayed in an errorview window as:

```
<—DIVISION BY ZERO—>
<—DIVISION BY ZERO—>
<—DIVISION BY ZERO—>
```

Since the selection is a property of a buffer, selecting an error message in an errorview window causes a BASEVIEW window to scroll to the given node. Using this feature, locations of errors in large buffers can be located rapidly.

2.7. Concrete Input Syntax

The input and output representations of a term are often closely related. However, in the interest of generality, SSL's mechanisms for defining them are separate and independent. Whereas Section 2.6 describes how the terms of a phylum are given a concrete output representation so that they can be displayed as text, this section describes how input text can be translated into terms.

The section is divided into six parts, describing the text-entry paradigm, entry declarations, parsing declarations, precedence declarations, lexical analysis, and a collection of examples, respectively.

2.7.1. The text-entry paradigm

During editing, each buffer has an associated *selection*, which is either a subtree or sublist of the buffer's contents. The selection is displayed according to the unparsing schemes of its constituent productions, as described in Section 2.6. The selection is either editable as text or immutable.

An immutable selection cannot be edited as text. Any attempt to delete or insert characters when the selection is immutable is prevented and an error message is issued. Note, however, that constituents of an immutable selection need not be immutable (*i.e.* they may be editable as text). In order to perform text editing on such a constituent, it is necessary to move the selection to the editable part.

In contrast, if a selection is editable as text, it can be modified character-by-character in the fashion of a conventional, display-oriented, text editor. When the user invokes a command to redirect the selection to a different part of the object, the text of the selection, as modified, is first parsed. If the text is not syntactically correct in the context of the current selection, the cursor is positioned near the first token that the parser did not accept, an error message is issued, and the command redirecting the selection is canceled. If the text is syntactically correct, then a term determined from the text replaces the currently selected term and the user's command is executed (which may move the selection to a new location).

Suppose the apex of the current selection is an operator of phylum p. Let s be the result of text editing the selection, or alternatively, let s be the contents of a text file read by the **insert-file** command. Then the following two-step process is used to translate s to a term t, which then replaces the current selection:

1) String s is parsed and a parse tree t' of phylum p' is produced. The mechanism for associating a concrete input language with a phylum such as p' will be described in Sections 2.7.3 – 2.7.5.

2) The parse tree t' is attributed and some designated attribute a of the root of t' provides the value t that replaces the currently selected term. After attribute $p'.a$ is extracted from t', the parse tree is thrown away.

There are several rationales for this two-step translation. First, by distinguishing between the parse trees of the parsing grammar and the abstract terms being edited, we are able to separate parsing concerns (*e.g.* is the grammar LALR(1), is it unambiguous, are the rules written in such a manner that the parse stack will not get too large) from those of the abstract syntax (*e.g.* does the abstract structure match the user's conception of the language, is it convenient for attribution). Second, it allows use of the full power of attribution in performing the translation. Third, it provides a way of handling input errors, since frequent errors can be parsed and then mapped to the appropriate (correct) abstract syntax. Fourth, it creates the possibility of designing input languages that are not restricted to the concrete display representation. That is, one may view the user's input text as a command to the editor to make an insertion.

Each of the two translation steps is context-sensitive in its own way:

1) The goal phylum p' for the parsing of s is specified as a function of p, the phylum of the apex of the current selection. That is, the parse tree t' depends on the "structural context" of the current selection.

2) In attributing the parse tree t' to obtain the replacement term t, attributes of p, the apex of the current selection, can be used to define inherited attributes of p', the root of the parse tree. That is, the replacement term t is determined, in part, as a function of the "context-sensitive context" at the selection.

See Section 3.5, "Entering and Editing an Object," Section 3.7, "Changing the Character Selection by Traversal of the Text Buffer," and Section 3.12, "Textual Editing" for further details on using the text-editing features of generated editors.

2.7.2. Entry declarations

Suppose the selection is a term or sublist of phylum p. In order for the selection to be editable as text, there must exist at least one *entry declaration* for p. Entry declarations have one of the following two forms:

> *abstract-syntax-phylum* ~ *concrete-syntax-phylum* . *attribute-name* ;
>
> *abstract-syntax-phylum* ~ *concrete-syntax-phylum* . *attribute-name*
>   { *equations* } ;

where *abstract-syntax-phylum* and *concrete-syntax-phylum* are phyla (the separate names merely reflecting their usage) and *attribute-name* is a synthesized attribute of *concrete-syntax-phylum*.

Such a declaration specifies that when the apex of the current selection in the abstract-syntax tree is a tree node of phylum *abstract-syntax-phylum*, input is to be parsed according to the parsing declarations of *concrete-syntax-phylum*, and the value of attribute *concrete-syntax-phylum.attribute-name* is to be inserted in the abstract-syntax tree to replace the currently selected subterm or sublist. The named attribute must have type *abstract-syntax-phylum*. In attributing the parse tree, any inherited attributes of *concrete-syntax-phylum* are defined in the {*equations*} section of the second form of entry declaration.

Thus, if we wish to specify that when the selection is a term of phylum p, text is to be parsed as a term of phylum p' and attribute $p'.a$ is to replace the selection, we write the declaration

p ~ $p'.a$;

and, if we wish inherited attribute i of p' to be defined as $p.b$, we would write the declaration

p ~ $p'.a$ { $p'.i = p.b$; };

Note that upward remote attribute sets in the attribute equations of the concrete input syntax and entry declarations may "pass through" entry declarations in order to refer to attributes in the abstract syntax. For this purpose, the entry declaration

abstract-syntax-phylum
  ~ *concrete-syntax-phylum* . *attribute-name* { *equations* } ;

is interpreted as if it were the production

abstract-syntax-phylum :
  operator-name (*concrete-syntax-phylum*) { *equations* } ;

where *operator-name* is some unique name generated by the compiler.

Example 2.7.2(a). In the desk calculator of Appendix A, the respective correspondences between phyla Calc and Exp of the concrete input syntax and phyla calc and exp of the abstract syntax are defined by the entry declarations

```
/* 68 */    calc ~ Calc.abs;
/* 69 */    exp ~ Exp.abs;
```

2.7.3. Parsing declarations

The first step in translating a string *s* is to create a parse tree *t'* of some given phylum *p'*. In this section and the two that follow, we explain how to associate concrete input languages with phyla in such a way that each string uniquely determines a parse tree.

In summary, each phylum *p'* is identified with a nonterminal in a context-free grammar known as the *concrete input grammar*, or, for short, IG. $L(p')$, the concrete input language associated with *p'*, is the set of strings that can be derived from *p'* using the productions of IG. The strings in $L(p')$ are sequences of characters, lexeme names, and special entry tokens. The productions of IG are defined in such a way that the terms of phylum *p'* can serve as parse trees for strings in $L(p')$. IG may be ambiguous, but can be augmented with precedence declarations for disambiguation. The productions of IG, together with the precedence rules, serve to define an LALR(1) parser.

The grammar IG is defined as follows:

1) The start symbol of IG is *YYentry*.
2) The nonterminal symbols of IG include *YYentry* and all phyla declared in the specification. Typically, only some of these participate in the productions of IG and the rest are irrelevant.
3) The terminal symbols of IG include all ASCII characters, all lexeme names (declared in the manner described in Section 2.2), and a special symbol *p_ENTRY* for each entry declaration with *p* on the left-hand side.
4) The productions of IG are defined in the paragraphs that follow. In summary, there is one production for each lexeme declaration, one for each parsing declaration (to be defined below) and one for each entry declaration. To differentiate the productions of IG from the corresponding SSL parsing declarations, we use the notation $A \to \alpha$, where *A* is a nonterminal symbol of IG and α is a sequence of terminal and nonterminal symbols of IG.

Recall, from Section 2.2, that the lexeme declaration

phylum-name : *lexeme-name* < *regular-expression* >;

specifies that the named phylum contains all strings in the regular set corresponding to the *regular-expression*. It also contributes the production

phylum-name → *lexeme-name*

to the concrete input grammar IG, where *lexeme-name* is one of the terminal symbols of IG. The regular expressions serve to define a lexical analyzer for arbitrary ASCII text, as described in Section 2.7.5.

The production declaration

phylum-name : *operator-name* (*phylum*$_1$ *phylum*$_2$ $\cdots$ *phylum*$_k$);

declares membership in *phylum-name* of the terms constructed by applying a *k*-ary operator *operator-name* to argument terms of the phyla *phylum*$_1$, *phylum*$_2$, ..., *phylum*$_k$. This form of declaration does not contribute any production to IG. However, an alternative form, known as a *parsing declaration*, defines a concrete input production for IG at the same time as the abstract operator is declared. A parsing declaration is signified by using the symbol ::= instead of : to separate left and right sides. Its form is

---

phylum-name ::=
    operator-name(*tokens phylum*$_1$ *tokens phylum*$_2$ $\cdots$ *phylum*$_k$ *tokens*);

---

where *tokens* are sequences of constants of type CHAR, as described in Section 2.2.1. Note that STR constants are *not* tokens. The production of IG defined by such a parsing declaration is

phylum-name → *tokens phylum*$_1$ *tokens phylum*$_2$ $\cdots$ *phylum*$_k$ *tokens*

The operator and terms defined by such a parsing declaration are exactly the same as if the declaration had been

phylum-name : *operator-name* (*phylum*$_1$ *phylum*$_2$ $\cdots$ *phylum*$_k$);

The terms of *phylum-name* are essentially parse trees for strings derived by IG from *phylum-name*. *Tokens* do not appear in the parse tree terms, since they are constants of the production and are, therefore, implicitly known. Note, however, that some of the *phylum*$_i$ may be lexical phyla. Since, in general, the lexeme represents a set of strings, knowing which particular string occurred in the input may be relevant. Therefore, the corresponding string does appear in the parse tree as the i-th argument of the operator.

Note that operator names of parse tree terms are usually not needed, since the parse trees are constructed by the parser. Therefore, the operator name is optional; it can be omitted and a unique operator name will be generated automatically.

As with other kinds of SSL declarations, when a number of parsing declarations are specified for a single phylum, the phylum can be factored to the left and the alternatives separated by vertical bars:

$$
\begin{array}{l}
\textit{phylum-name} ::= \\
\quad\quad \textit{operator-name} (\textit{parsing-scheme}) \\
\quad | \quad \textit{operator-name} (\textit{parsing-scheme}) \\
\quad \ldots \\
\quad | \quad \textit{operator-name} (\textit{parsing-scheme}) \\
\quad ;
\end{array}
$$

Such a declaration defines a concrete input production for each alternative, as described above. Attribution equations for the phyla of the concrete input syntax can be defined separately or can be combined with the parsing declarations using the following syntax:

$$
\begin{array}{l}
\textit{phylum-name} ::= \\
\quad\quad \textit{operator-name} (\textit{parsing-scheme}) \{ \textit{equations} \} \\
\quad | \quad \textit{operator-name} (\textit{parsing-scheme}) \{ \textit{equations} \} \\
\quad \ldots \\
\quad | \quad \textit{operator-name} (\textit{parsing-scheme}) \{ \textit{equations} \} \\
\quad ;
\end{array}
$$

For each entry declaration

$$p \sim p' . a ;$$

the following production is contributed to IG:

$$\textit{YYentry} \rightarrow p\_ENTRY\ p'$$

The purpose of this production is to provide an "entry point" into the parser for IG. When the current editor selection is a term of phylum p, and when p has entry declaration

$$p \sim p' . a \; ;$$

we treat p' as if it were a root symbol to which the input string is to be reduced. This is accomplished by first prepending the symbol p_ENTRY to the input string. The parser can then reduce the input, thus modified, to the grammar's true root symbol, *YYentry*.

2.7.4. Ambiguity and precedence declarations

The SSL compiler makes use of the yacc parser generator [Johnson78] to construct an LALR(1) parser for IG. Ambiguities in the productions of IG are detected by yacc and reported as reduce/reduce conflicts and shift/reduce conflicts. By default, such conflicts are resolved according to the following rules:

1) For a shift/reduce conflict, perform the shift.
2) For a reduce/reduce conflict, reduce by the production associated with the declaration appearing earliest in the specification.

Precedence declarations provide an additional mechanism for dealing with ambiguous grammars. Such declarations associate precedence levels with characters, lexemes, and productions of IG. Three forms of precedence declarations define precedence levels of characters and lexemes:

```
left token-or-phylum₁, . . . , token-or-phylumₖ ;
right token-or-phylum₁, . . . , token-or-phylumₖ ;
nonassoc token-or-phylum₁, . . . , token-or-phylumₖ ;
```

Each *token-or-phylum* is either a CHAR constant (*e.g.* 'a') or the name of a lexical phylum (*e.g.* INTEGER). A *token-or-phylum* that is a phylum name denotes the set of lexeme alternatives of that phylum.

Each instance of such a declaration assigns the same precedence level and the same associativity to all characters and lexemes denoted by *token-or-phylum₁*, . . . , *token-or-phylumₖ*. The precedence levels increase for each successive declaration, *i.e.* the character and lexemes denoted bind increasingly tightly.

A production of IG (arising from a parsing declaration) can be given a precedence level explicitly by using a parsing declaration of the form

phylum-name ::=
  operator-name (*list-of-tokens-and-phyla* **prec** *token-or-phylum*) ;

It assigns the corresponding production of IG the same precedence level as the character or lexemes denoted by *token-or-phylum*.

The parser produced by yacc on behalf of the SSL compiler uses precedences and associativities of characters, lexemes, and productions to resolve parsing conflicts. The disambiguation rules, quoted below from the yacc manual, are paraphrased to match the vocabulary of SSL:

1) Precedences and associativities are recorded for those characters and lexemes that have been assigned them.

2) Productions derived from parsing declarations with the **prec** option are assigned the precedence and associativity of the character token or the lexemes denoted by the *token-or-phylum*. Productions derived from parsing declarations without the **prec** option are assigned the precedence of the last token (*i.e.* CHAR constant) of the production. Productions not containing any tokens or **prec** option have no precedence or associativity. Entry declarations have no precedence or associativity.

3) When there is a reduce/reduce conflict, or there is a shift/reduce conflict and either the input symbol (*i.e.* character or lexeme name) or the grammar rule has no precedence and associativity, the two disambiguation rules given in Section 2.7.3 are used and the conflicts are reported.

4) If there is a shift/reduce conflict, and both grammar rule and input character have precedence and associativity, the conflict is resolved in favor of the action (shift or reduce) associated with the higher precedence. If precedences are the same, associativity is used: left associative implies reduce; right associative implies shift; nonassociating implies error.

In the event of parsing conflicts, the compiler error messages will be those of yacc. To debug parsing conflicts, use the −v flag of sgen, which directs yacc to create a file named y.output containing detailed and useful diagnostics.

Example 2.7.4(a). This example illustrates an important difference between yacc and SSL in connection with rule 2) above. Yacc implicitly assigns precedence to productions according to the precedence of the last "token" in the production, where yacc's notion of token includes both character constants and symbols declared to be tokens. Thus, in yacc, if POWER were declared a token, for example, by the rules

```
%token POWER            /* the yacc token "**" for exponentiation. */
%left POWER
```

the production

```
Exp:    Exp POWER Exp ;
```

would implicitly be assigned the precedence and associativity of token
POWER. The corresponding SSL declaration of POWER is

```
POWER: <   "**"  >;
left  POWER;
```

However, SSL parsing declarations are implicitly assigned a precedence only if
they contain an SSL token, *i.e.* a constant of type CHAR, for example

```
Exp::= (Exp '+' Exp) ;
```

is assigned the precedence of '+', but

```
Exp::= (Exp POWER Exp) ;
```

is not assigned any precedence. To assign the precedence of POWER to the
given parsing declaration, the prec option must be used:

```
Exp ::= (Exp POWER Exp   prec POWER) ;
```


2.7.5. Lexical analysis

The ordered collection of regular expressions appearing in lexeme declarations,
serve to define the lexical analyzer used by the parser. Each regular expression
denotes a set of strings. Each time the parser requires a new input symbol, the
remaining input text is matched against these regular expressions and the lexeme name containing the longest prefix of the input text is returned. In the event
of a tie, the lexeme name declared earlier in the specification is returned. In the
event that no declared lexeme name matches the input, the next character is
returned as a single-character token.

Phylum WHITESPACE has special significance. Whenever the matching
lexeme is derived from WHITESPACE, it is consumed within the lexical
analyzer and scanning resumes. Lexemes for WHITESPACE are not
predefined; rather, a suitable lexeme declaration must appear in the SSL
specification. The following declaration is sufficient for most purposes:

```
WHITESPACE: < [\ \t\n]  >;
```

In scanning input text, a degree of sensitivity to left context can be obtained by exploiting *scanner state*. Scanner state is controlled in the following manner. Each time the parser is invoked, the state is initialized according to the *<start-state>* field of the operative entry declaration:

> *abstract-syntax-phylum ~*
>   *<start-state> concrete-syntax-phylum.attribute-name* ;

If the entry declaration contains no *<start-state>* field or if the parser is invoked by the **read-file** command, the scanner is initialized in the distinguished state INITIAL.

Recognition of certain lexemes causes the scanner to change state. In particular, recognizing a lexeme whose declaration is

> *phylum-name* : *lexeme-name< regular-expression <final-state> >;*

causes the scanner to change to the given *final-state*. If a lexeme declaration contains no *<final-state>* field, the state is not changed.

By restricting lexeme declarations to have effect only in certain states, scanner state is used to control the recognition process. In particular, a lexeme declaration of the form

> *phylum-name* : *lexeme-name< <start-state> regular-expression >;*

is enabled only when the scanner is in the given *start-state*. That is, unless the scanner is in the given *start-state*, the lexeme declaration has no effect. In general, a lexeme declaration with no *<start-state>* field is always enabled.

A lexeme declaration can have both *<start-state>* and *<final-state>* fields:

> *phylum-name* :
>   *lexeme-name< <start-state> regular-expression <final-state> >;*

It is essential to separate the *<final-state>* field from the *regular-expression* by at least one blank. State names are identifiers.

2.7.6. Examples

This section contains a collection of examples that illustrate the definition of concrete input syntax.

Example 2.7.6(a). The following rules define a concrete input syntax for the desk calculator of Appendix A. The phyla Calc and Exp are used for parsing text corresponding to the abstract phyla calc and exp, respectively. The attribution rules of Calc and Exp synthesize, in attribute abs, the appropriate abstract term of phylum calc or exp. Note that in the course of this translation, each INTEGER (a textual lexeme) becomes an INT (a number).

```
/* 46 */    /* Lexical syntax */
/* 47 */    INTEGER: < [0–9]+ >;
/* 48 */    WHITESPACE: < [\ \t\n] >;
/* 49 */
/* 50 */    /* Parse syntax */
/* 51 */    Calc { synthesized calc abs; };
/* 52 */    Exp { synthesized exp abs; };
/* 53 */
/* 54 */    left '+', '–';
/* 55 */    left '*', '/';
/* 56 */
/* 57 */    Calc::= (Exp)    { Calc.abs = CalcPair(Exp.abs, CalcNil()); }
/* 58 */       | (Exp  Calc) { Calc$1.abs = CalcPair(Exp.abs, Calc$2.abs); }
/* 59 */       ;
/* 60 */    Exp::= (INTEGER) { $$.abs = Const(STRtoINT(INTEGER)); }
/* 61 */       | (Exp '+' Exp)   { $$.abs = Sum( Exp$2.abs, Exp$3.abs); }
/* 62 */       | (Exp '–' Exp)   { $$.abs = Diff(Exp$2.abs, Exp$3.abs); }
/* 63 */       | (Exp '*' Exp)   { $$.abs = Prod(Exp$2.abs, Exp$3.abs); }
/* 64 */       | (Exp '/' Exp)   { $$.abs = Quot(Exp$2.abs, Exp$3.abs); }
/* 65 */       | ('(' Exp ')')   { $$.abs = Exp$2.abs; }
/* 66 */       ;
```

Example 2.7.6(b). Input text to be parsed need not be a fragment of the concrete display language of the editor; rather, we may treat it as a command in a user-defined command language. This possibility is illustrated by adding such a command to the desk calculator of Appendix A. We intend that typing (and parsing) text of the form

name =

is to have the effect of inserting a let-expression with the given *name* already filled in. For example, typing x= when the selection is <exp>, will insert

```
let x = <exp> in
  <exp>
ni
```

The following four lines, when added to the desk calculator specification, are sufficient to implement the new command:

```
ExpCommand { synthesized exp abs; };
exp ~ ExpCommand.abs;
ExpCommand ::= (ID '=')
  { ExpCommand.abs = Let(Def(ID),<Exp>,<Exp>); };
```

Example 2.7.6(c). Attributes of the selection apex in the abstract tree can be inherited into the parse tree and used to determine the translation of input text. To illustrate this feature, we implement a new desk-calculator command whose translation requires access to the environment attribute. Typing (and parsing) text of the form

.name

is to have the effect of inserting the value of the given *name* as bound in the environment of the current selection. The following lines implement the new command:

```
ExpCommand { inherited ENV env; };
exp ~ ExpCommand.abs  { ExpCommand.env = exp.env; };
ExpCommand ::= ('.' ID)
    { ExpCommand.abs =
        let Binding(*,i)=lookup(ID, ExpCommand.env) in (Const(i));
    };
```

In the entry declaration above, exp.env refers to the environment attribute of the exp phylum at the apex of the selection when the command *.name* is typed. In an editor for a Pascal-like language, templates that depend on a program's type declarations or procedure declarations could be defined in a similar fashion.

2.8. Transformation Declarations

During editing, each buffer has an associated *selection*, either a subtree or sub-list of the buffer's contents. *Transformation declarations* specify editor commands for restructuring the selection. The form of a transformation declaration is

---

transform *phylum* on *transformation-name pattern* : *expression* ;

---

where *transformation-name* is any (quoted) STR constant. The type of the *expression* must be the given *phylum*.

The transformation declarations whose patterns match the current selection are termed the *enabled transformations* of the buffer. Pattern matching is exactly as defined in Section 2.5.6, with the sole exception that as clauses are not currently implemented. For the purpose of pattern matching, a sublist selection is considered to end with the appropriate nullary operator of the list phylum.

If the patterns of several transformations with the same name match the selection, then only one with that name is enabled — the one appearing earliest in the specification. When the selection is a singleton sublist, the enabled transformations also include those that would have matched had the selection been just the item of the sublist. If two patterns with the same name match, one for the list phylum and the other for the item phylum, the transformation for the list phylum takes precedence.

The set of transformation names associated with the enabled transformations constitute the *enabled transformation commands*, which are displayed in the help pane of each window. In editors generated for workstations with bit-mapped displays, the list of enabled transformation commands also appears in a pop-up menu. Section 3.2, "Executing Commands and Transformations," describes how transformations are invoked. In summary, there are three ways:

1) By invoking **execute-command** and typing the *transformation-name* followed by a space or some key-sequence bound to a command. Note that it will not be possible to invoke a transformation whose *transformation-name* includes spaces or key-sequences that are bound to commands.
2) By clicking on the *transformation-name* in the help pane (in editors generated for workstations equipped with a mouse).
3) By selecting the transformation from the appropriate pop-up menu (in editors generated for workstations equipped with a mouse).

Invoking one of the enabled transformations causes the selection to be replaced with the value of the associated expression. The expression is evaluated in an environment in which the pattern's pattern variables are bound to constituents of the selection according to the pattern match. After a transformation has been applied and the selection replaced, the values of the buffer's attributes are updated, as necessary, so that all attributes are again consistent with their definitions.

Since the selection is not merely a term, but is an attributed term, pattern variables are necessarily bound to attributed terms. If pattern variable p is bound to a term with synthesized or inherited attribute a, the expression $p.a$ is legitimate within the transformation *expression* and denotes the value of attribute a. (Note: this feature should not be used when the selection is a sublist and evaluation of $p.a$ may result in evaluating demand attributes.)

If a pattern variable occurs more than once within the *expression*, the constituent of the selection bound to that pattern variable will, in effect, be replicated. Any pattern variable never occurring in the *expression* denotes a constituent of the selection that will be lost when the transformation is applied. Similarly, occurrences of * and default in a pattern will be bound to components that will disappear as a result of the transformation.

As with other kinds of SSL declarations, when a number of transformation declarations are specified for a single phylum, the phylum can be factored to the left:

---

transform *phylum*
    on *transformation-name*$_1$ *pattern*$_1$: *expression*$_1$,
    on *transformation-name*$_2$ *pattern*$_2$: *expression*$_2$,

    . . .

    on *transformation-name*$_k$ *pattern*$_k$: *expression*$_k$

    ;

Example 2.8(a). The following transformation declarations define templates for inserting arithmetic operators at an unexpanded exp.

```
/* 40 */   transform exp on "+" <exp> : Sum ( <exp>, <exp> ),
/* 41 */              on "–" <exp> : Diff ( <exp>, <exp> ),
/* 42 */              on "*" <exp> : Prod ( <exp>, <exp> ),
/* 43 */              on "/" <exp> : Quot ( <exp>, <exp> )
/* 44 */              ;
```

Example 2.8(b). The following rules define transformations for restructuring expressions according to the commutative and distributive laws of arithmetic. The transformation named evaluate has the effect of replacing an expression with its value.

```
/* 72 */   transform exp
/* 73 */      on "factor-left" Sum(Prod(a,b),Prod(a,c)): Prod(a,Sum(b,c)),
/* 74 */      on "factor-right" Sum(Prod(b,a),Prod(c,a)): Prod(Sum(b,c),a),
/* 75 */      on "distribute-left" Prod(a,Sum(b,c)): Sum(Prod(a,b),Prod(a,c)),
/* 76 */      on "distribute-right" Prod(Sum(b,c),a): Sum(Prod(b,a),Prod(c,a)),
/* 77 */      on "commute" Sum(a,b): Sum(b,a),
/* 78 */      on "commute" Prod(a,b): Prod(b,a),
/* 79 */      on "evaluate" t: Const(t.v)
/* 80 */      ;
```

2.9. Support for Modular Specifications

To support modular specifications of editors, the declarations concerning separate aspects of a language can be placed in separate portions of a specification. Such modularity enhances the comprehensibility of editor specifications; it also facilitates the generation of a collection of related editors that offer different degrees of static-semantic analysis for different language dialects.

It is the ability to augment a specification with new properties that permits specifications to be factored. In particular, it is possible to extend the attribute-grammar component in three ways:

1) by adding a new attribute to a phylum declared previously;
2) by adding new attribute equations to productions declared previously;
3) by adding new operators and their attribute equations to a phylum declared previously.

Furthermore, it is possible to define additional styles, views, transformations, and so forth. As described in Section 2.2.2, the interpretation of regular expressions for lexical analysis depends on the order in which they appear in a specification. Therefore, one must be careful to order lexeme declarations appropriately when combining specifications.

In Appendix A, lines 71-158 extend the previous rules with the abstract syntax and attribute equations for let clauses and the use of bound names.

Under some circumstances, it may be desirable to group all declarations for a given phylum together. The most general form of phylum declaration permits the declarations of operators, their attribute equations, and their unparsing scheme all within the same alternative of a phylum declaration.

> *phylum-name* :
>
>   *operator-list*(*parameters*) { *equations* } [*unparsing-scheme*]
>
> | *operator-list*(*parameters*) { *equations* } [*unparsing-scheme*]
>
>   . . .
>
> | *operator-list*(*parameters*) { *equations* } [*unparsing-scheme*]
>
>   ;

In addition, {*equations*} and [*unparsing-scheme*] may occur multiple times and can be intermixed.

2.10. Option Declarations

Option declarations provide the means to set options in SSL. The form of an option declaration is:

> let *compile-time-option-name* = *constant* ;

Presently, there is only one option:

format_strings
>   Formatting commands in STR values are interpreted during unparsing if and only if this variable is true. Default: false.

2.11. Quantified Declarations

Quantified declarations provide a limited degree of polymorphism in SSL. The construct

```
forall phylum-name₁ , ... , phylum-nameₙ in
   list-of-quantified-declarations
end ;
```

introduces a scope within which $phylum\text{-}name_1$, ..., $phylum\text{-}name_n$ are declared parameters that range over all possible phyla. Any name following forall can be preceded by the keyword list, in which case the range of the given parameter is restricted to phyla that are declared with the list property. Quantified declarations are restricted to SSL function declarations, foreign function declarations, and primitive-phylum declarations. Any parameter phylum in the result type of a function declaration must appear in one of the parameter types of the function. Parameter phyla cannot be used within the body of functions.

Example 2.11(a). The following declaration defines the polymorphic identity function Id:

```
forall alpha in
   alpha Id(alpha x) { x };
end;
```

Example 2.11(b). The main use of quantified declarations is in the definition of new primitive phyla and the foreign functions that operate on such values. For example, the parameterized phylum TABLE and the foreign functions that operate on tables are declared in atoms.ssl as follows:

```
forall list L in
   TABLE[L]: Table =hashtable= ;
   TABLE[L] foreign MakeTable(L , INT j);
   L foreign Lookup(TABLE[L] t, STR k);
   L foreign UnmakeTable(TABLE[L] t);
end;
```

See Sections 5.1 and 5.2 for further details on foreign functions and the declaration of new primitive phyla.

CHAPTER 3

Using an Editor

Each different SSL specification results in an editor with distinct language-dependent characteristics; however, all generated editors share the generic user interface described in this chapter.

There is an obvious similarity between many of the features described below and the EMACS text editor [Stallman81]. In the interest of minimizing barriers to entry for this substantial population, EMACS command names and standard key-bindings have been adopted for similar or identical concepts.

3.1. Getting Into and Out of an Editor

An editor is created by the sgen command, as described in Appendix B. By default, the executable load module created by sgen is named syn.out. More descriptive names are typically assigned using the −o *filename* flag.

An editor can be invoked either with or without parameters. The parameter list specifies a collection of files to be loaded into editor buffers with corresponding names. If invoked with no arguments, editing begins in a default buffer named main with no associated file.

An editor that has been loaded with the debugger can be invoked with the −d flag, in which case execution will immediately stop in the debugger, thereby permitting the setting of breakpoints, *etc*. See Chapter 4 for a description of debugger features.

After loading all files to be edited, file .syn_profile is sought, first in the current working directory, and then in the user's home directory. If found, this file is loaded into buffer ParametersForm and serves to initialize the editor's parameters. Editor parameters are described in Section 3.2 under **set-parameters**; instructions for creating file .syn_profile appear there as well.

The windows of an editor are divided into four horizontal stripes — from top to bottom, the *title bar*, the *command line*, the *object pane*, and the *help pane*. The highlighted title bar gives the name of the buffer being displayed in the window; the command line contains echoed commands and error messages; the object pane displays the object being edited in the given window; the help pane lists the currently enabled transformations. A sample window, running the desk calculator of Appendix A, might appear as

```
 ┌─────────────────────────────────────────────────────┐
 │┌─────┐                                               │
 ││main │                                               │
 │└─────┘                                               │
 │                                                       │
 │┌─────┐                                                │
 ││<exp>│                                                │
 │└─────┘                                                │
 │VALUE = 0;                                             │
 │                                                       │
 │(2 /<—DIVISION BY ZERO—>(7 – 7))                       │
 │VALUE = 2;                                             │
 │Positioned at calc   +   –   *   /   evaluate   let    │
 └─────────────────────────────────────────────────────┘
```

Windows on workstations equipped with a mouse also have two scroll bars: one to the right of the object pane and the other below the object pane.

A running editor is terminated by executing the command **exit**, described in Section 3.2. Normally, **exit** is bound to ˆC.

Further details specific to particular workstations and window systems are described in Appendix D.

3.2. Executing Commands and Transformations

Every command of an editor has a *name* and zero or more *key-bindings*. Commands are invoked in one of four ways.

First, a sequence of keystrokes bound to the command may be typed. Second, the command may be selected from a menu. Third, an actuator bound to the command may be selected by mouse click. Fourth, the command name may be typed on the command line of a window. All keystrokes other than command key-bindings or escaped text entered on the command line are interpreted as textual insertions into the object being edited. To enter a command name on the command line, one first invokes **execute-command**, normally bound to TAB.

The window from which a command has been invoked is an implicit parameter of many commands. In editors generated for mouse-based window systems, the value of this parameter is the window containing the locator at the time the command is invoked. In editors generated for video-display terminals, explicit commands are provided for switching between windows. (See Section 3.4.)

If a command requires explicit parameters, these parameters are entered into a *parameter form* that appears on the screen as soon as the command is executed. (The one exception is **execute-command**, whose parameter is entered on the command line.) A parameter form is a structured object, and parameters should be entered by editing it like any other buffer. Depending on the particular parameter form, certain fields may be reinitialized on subsequent invocations while other fields may retain their contents from a previous command invocation. After the parameters have been entered, the command is passed its parameters by executing **start-command**. A command can be canceled at any time during the editing of its parameters by executing **cancel-command**. In mouse-based window systems, parameter forms contain actuators, labeled start and cancel, bound to **start-command** and **cancel-command**, respectively.

The commands described in this reference manual are incorporated in every generated editor. In addition, each specific editor provides a collection of transformation commands, as described in Section 2.8. Whereas the built-in commands are available in every context, transformations are enabled dynamically depending on the success of a pattern match at the current selection of the buffer. The list of enabled transformations is maintained in the help pane of each window. A transformation is invoked in the same way as a built-in command, namely, by escaping to the command line and typing its name. Alternatively, in editors generated for mouse-based systems, transformations can be selected from a menu. Transformations do not have associated key-bindings.

Each command is described in the sections below. The default key-bindings for a command are listed to the right of its name and parameters (if any). Some commands have no default key-bindings. Note the following standard labels for control keys:

^H   BACKSPACE
^I   TAB
^J   LINE-FEED
^M   RETURN

See Appendix D, "Keyboards, Displays, Window Systems, and Mice" for information on customizing key-bindings and for other workstation-specific information.

exit   ^C, ESC-^C, ^X^C

Leave the editor and return to the shell. A warning is issued if any buffers have been modified since their associated files were last written out. Such a warning appears in a form, as described above. To abort the **exit**, issue a **cancel-command**. To consummate the **exit**, issue a **start-command**.

execute-command *name*   ^I, ESC-x

Echo COMMAND: on the command line to signify command mode and redirect subsequent characters to the command line. Entry on the command line is terminated by the first blank, carriage return, or other command key-binding. The command name need not be typed in its entirety; any prefix of a command that uniquely identifies the command is sufficient. Transformations take priority over built-in commands. If the command has no parameters, it is executed immediately. Otherwise, a form for parameters appears; after the parameters have been provided, the command should be initiated by executing **start-command**. If a command parameter is either invalid or ambiguous, an error message is issued. In addition, if editor parameter help-on-command-error is on, then a help buffer containing likely command completions is created in a separate window. Note that the control character ^I is TAB.

illegal-operation   ^G, ESC-^G, ^X^G

Cancel any incomplete command key-binding or partial entry on the command line.

start-command   ESC-s

Initiate execution of a command with the parameters contained in the current form. If not currently editing a parameter form, **start-command** does nothing.

cancel-command   ESC-c

Cancel execution of the command awaiting completion of its parameter form. If not currently editing a parameter form, **cancel-command** does nothing.

execute-monitor-command *command-line*   ^X!

Pass the given *command-line* to UNIX to be executed as a command. Put the output of the execution in a textfile buffer, and place the buffer in a window other than the current window, if possible.

repeat-command   ESC-r

Repeat the most recently initiated command. If that command had parameters, repeat it with the same parameters.

return-to-monitor

Recursively call the UNIX shell. To return from the shell, type exit. In editors generated for window systems in which a separate shell window is

easily arranged, the **return-to-monitor** command is unnecessary. In editors
generated for video-display terminals, the **return-to-monitor** command provides access to a shell without the overhead of re-reading and re-analyzing
files.

set-parameters

Modify the global parameters of the editor. Execution of **set-parameters**
presents a form containing the current value of each editor parameter. The
parameters are changed by editing this form and then executing **start-
command**.

As discussed in Section 3.1, initial editor parameters can be loaded from a
file named .syn_profile. To create such a file, (a) invoke **switch-to-buffer**
ParametersForm, (b) edit the entries in this buffer, filling in all parameter
values, as desired, and (c) invoke **write-current-file**.

The global editing parameters are:

indentation

The number of spaces for each level of indenting in the display of structured objects. Default: 2.

help-height

The initial height of the help pane of a new window. Note that to change
the height of the help pane of an existing window, you must use the
enlarge-help or **shrink-help** command. Default: 4.

help-on-command-error

When an ambiguous system command name is typed, a list of possible
intended commands is displayed. This feature is disabled when help-
on-command-error is off. Default: on.

absolute-right-margin

The maximum number of numeric characters (*e.g.* 0's) displayed on a
line. Default: 32767

word-wrapping

If on, then the display of a term is adjusted so that no text extends
beyond the right margin of the display window. If off, text lines can be
wider than the window and are clipped. Default: on.

tab-stops

Number of numeric characters (*e.g.* 0's) between tab stops. Default: 8.

automatic-window-placement

If on, new windows are positioned automatically; if off, users position
new windows manually. This parameter is specific to editors generated
for the X Window System. Default: on.

apropos *keyword*   ESC-?

All commands containing the given keyword as a syllable or as a prefix of a
syllable are listed. The "syllables" of a command name are the sequences of
characters separated by hyphens.

3.3. Buffers, Selections, and Files

The objects manipulated in an editor are contained in a collection of named
buffers. Typically, each file being edited is read into a distinct buffer. The
buffer is then associated with the given file until either a different file is read
into that buffer, or the given buffer is written out to a different file.

Each buffer has an associated *syntactic mode*, one of the phyla declared in the
editor specification. Typically, this is the root phylum of the grammar, as
described in Section 2.2.5. However, a buffer may be created with arbitrary
syntactic mode using the **new-buffer** command. Phylum textfile is predefined
and is the syntactic mode of buffers consisting of zero or more lines of text.

Each buffer of syntactic mode *phy* contains a term of phylum *phy*, known as
the *value* of the buffer. The editor guarantees that, as the buffer is edited, its
value remains a syntactically well-formed term in phylum *phy*. Operations on
the buffer are defined according to the structure of this term and the current
selection of the buffer. The *selection*, indicated on the display by highlighting,
is a subterm or sublist of the term.

Several buffers are distinguished. Buffer CLIPPED is used for cutting and
pasting of fragments. It contains the fragment most recently removed by **cut-
to-clipped** or copied by **copy-to-clipped**. The syntactic mode of CLIPPED
changes with each **cut-to-clipped** or **copy-to-clipped** command.

Buffer DELETED is used for deleting fragments. It contains the fragment
most recently removed by **delete-selection**. Although CLIPPED can also be
used for deletion, CLIPPED and DELETED are frequently used in concert to
extract a constituent from its enclosing structure and discard the enclosing structure.

Direct editing of buffers CLIPPED and DELETED is not permitted.

Three file *formats* are supported: *text*, *structure*, and *attributed*. A text file
contains the display representation of a term; a structure file contains an internal
representation of a term (without attributes); and an attributed file contains an
internal representation of an attributed term.

Most file-writing commands write the contents of a single buffer. The buffer
to be written is the one displayed in the window that contains the cursor at the
time the file-writing command is issued. Suppose this buffer contains term t.
Further suppose that the window is displaying term t in view v. If written as

text, the file will contain exactly the same array of characters as would appear
for *t* in a view *v* window infinitely high and as wide as the current setting of the
editor's **absolute-right-margin** parameter. If written in either structure or attributed format, the entire term *t* is written regardless of whether the view is
sparse or dense.

Commands **write-modified-files** and **write-file-exit** each write the contents of
all modified buffers that have an associated file and file format. These commands always write text files according to the BASEVIEW display representation.

A term written as a structure or attributed file can always be read back into an
editor; the unparsing schemes in effect at the time the file was written are
recorded in the file and are restored. In contrast, a text file can only be read
back into an editor if the text can be reparsed; unparsing schemes in effect at the
time a text file was written are not restored.

list-buffers   ˆXˆB

List all buffers and their associated properties in a textfile buffer and place
that buffer in a window other than the current window, if possible.

switch-to-buffer *buffer-name*   ˆXb

Place the named buffer in the current window. If no such buffer exists,
create a new buffer. The new buffer is associated with the root phylum of
the grammar, and is initialized with the placeholder term of that phylum.

new-buffer *buffer-name phylum*

Create a new buffer with the given name. If there is already a buffer with
that name, the command is invalid. The new buffer has the given phylum as
its associated syntactic mode, and is initialized with the placeholder term of
that phylum. Place the new buffer in the current window.

read-file *file-name*   ˆXˆF, ˆXˆR

Read a named file into the current buffer, deleting the previous contents of
that buffer. The buffer becomes associated with the file for subsequent
write-current-file commands. If the current buffer is already associated
with a file that has not been written since the buffer was last updated, you
must fill in yes in the field of the parameter form labeled Overwrite buffer?
before the read will be executed. If the file to be read is text, it must be syntactically correct with respect to the input syntax of the given editor. If syntactically incorrect, the file is read into a text buffer with the character selection positioned near the error. If the file is structured or attributed, it must
contain a term of the phylum that is the syntactic mode of the buffer. If the
file is attributed, the attributes from the file can be discarded and recomputed
by filling in no in the field of the parameter form labeled Read attributes

from file? (This option is useful when one wishes to read an old attributed file with a new version of an editor.)

visit-file *file-name*   ˆXˆV

Read a named file into a buffer with the corresponding name. If a buffer already exists with that name, a new buffer is created with that name suffixed by *<i>*, for some distinct integer *i*. The **visit-file** command is otherwise identical to the **read-file** command.

write-current-file   ˆXs

Write the value of the buffer displayed in the current window to its associated file in the current format associated with the buffer.

write-named-file *file-name format*   ˆXˆW

Write the value of the buffer displayed in the current window to the given file in the given format. The default format, attributed, can be changed by selecting the *format* field of the parameter form and invoking either the text or structure transformation.

write-modified-files   ˆXˆM

Write the contents of every modified buffer to its associated file in the current format associated with the buffer.

write-file-exit   ˆXf

Write the contents of every modified buffer to its associated file in the current format associated with the buffer and then exit the editor.

insert-file *file-name*   ˆXˆI

Replace the current selection of the buffer with the contents of the given file. Note that only the selection is replaced, not the entire buffer contents. If the given file is text, it must be syntactically correct with respect to the input syntax at the current selection. If syntactically incorrect, the file is read into a text buffer with the character selection positioned near the error. If the given file is a structure or attributed file, the term contained in the file must be in the phylum of the current selection.

write-selection-to-file *file-name format*

Write the current selection to the given file in the given format. Note that only the selection is written, not the entire buffer contents.

3.4. Creating, Deleting, and Resizing Windows and Panes

In editors generated for video-display terminals, windows are non-overlapping, are arranged in horizontal stripes across the screen, and are cyclicly ordered from top to bottom for the purpose of the **next-window** and **previous-window** commands.

In editors generated for workstations with high-resolution, bitmapped displays, resizable and overlapping windows with scroll bars are supported. See Appendix D for further details.

split-current-window   ^X2
> Create a new window and display the same buffer in both windows. The new window presents the same view as the original window. Although a buffer has but one selection, each window displaying a buffer can be independently scrolled.

change-view *view-name*
> Change the display view of the current window.

delete-other-windows   ^X1
> Delete all windows other than the current one.

delete-window   ^Xd
> Delete the current window. In editors generated for video-display terminals, the previous window becomes the current window.

enlarge-window   ^Xz
> Increase the height of the current window by one line, if possible. (Video-display terminals only.)

shrink-window   ^X^Z
> Decrease the height of the current window by one line, if possible. (Video-display terminals only.)

next-window   ^Xn
> Switch to the next window on the screen. (Video-display terminals only.)

previous-window   ^Xp
> Switch to the previous window on the screen. (Video-display terminals only.)

help-off
> Reduce the height of the help pane of the current window to zero.

help-on
> Reset the size of the help pane of the current window to the default size.

enlarge-help   ESC-^Xz
> Increase the size of the help pane of the current window by one line.

shrink-help   ESC-^X^Z
> Decrease the size of the help pane of the current window by one line.

redraw-display   ^L
> Refresh the screen image to remove any spurious characters.

3.5. Entering and Editing an Object

A newly created buffer of syntactic mode *phy* contains the placeholder term of that phylum. In general, after some editing has occurred, the buffer contains a term with several placeholders. The buffer is modified by successively replacing constituent subterms in arbitrary order. Typically, entry proceeds by replacing placeholders by new constituents. These replacement terms may be created by invoking transformations, by moving or copying fragments from elsewhere, or by typing in new input text.

Template-insertion commands may be provided among the transformations. A template insertion is, in effect, the transformation of a placeholder into a term that contains other placeholders or completing terms. Such commands provide a simple and safe way to insert language fragments, and are described in Section 2.8. The menu of enabled transformations is maintained in the help pane of each window. Section 3.2 describes how to select transformations for execution.

Commands to insert fragments moved or copied from elsewhere are described in Section 3.11. The command **insert-file**, which inserts a fragment read from a file, is described in Section 3.3.

Textual entry is permitted at some selections and forbidden at others, depending on the specifics of the particular generated editor. For text editing to be permitted, there must be an entry declaration for the phylum of the selection, as described in Section 2.7. In addition, the unparsing scheme must specify that text editing is permitted, as described in Section 2.6. Any attempt to type characters while positioned at a selection where text entry is not permitted is prevented and an error message is issued.

Suppose that textual entry is permitted at a given placeholder. Then, when the first character is typed, the unparsed text of the placeholder is replaced on the screen by the character typed. Typed text is collected in a *text buffer*, which is displayed in place, exactly where the placeholder was displayed. The editor then behaves as a normal full-screen text editor within this context. A text buffer contains a *character selection* in front of which character insertions and deletions occur. On video displays, the character selection is denoted on the screen as an unhighlighted character within the highlighted text buffer. On bit-mapped displays, the character selection is the character to the right of the symbol $\mathbf{I}$ that appears whenever a text buffer is present. A text buffer may contain multiple lines. The command **new-line** inserts a new line in the text buffer without invoking syntactic analysis.

The entered text is analyzed as soon as the selection is redirected away from the entered fragment. If the text cannot be parsed according to the rules pro-

vided by the editor designer for the given context, an error message is provided
and the selection is positioned on the rightmost character of the first token that
cannot be interpreted. The syntax error must be corrected at this time and, in
fact, no other editing operations can be performed until the correction is made.

If the text parses successfully, the current selection is replaced by a term produced by attributing the parse tree. The mechanism for performing this translation is described in Section 2.7, "Concrete Input Syntax." After successful
analysis, the display is regenerated from the abstract form. Therefore, upon
analysis, appearances may change; for example, redundant parentheses may
disappear. Alternatively, the editor designer may have provided parsing rules
that make sense of incomplete input, in which case missing pieces may be provided automatically.

Suppose that the selection is not a placeholder but is some production at
which textual editing is permitted. Then, upon the first keystroke implying a
textual modification, the display representation of the selection is captured into a
text buffer. Operations within the selection are then defined textually, not structurally. The character string in the text buffer is analyzed as soon as the selection is redirected outside of the textual region, exactly as if the text had been
entered from scratch. Although font sizes and characteristics are maintained in
text buffers, they have no effect on parsing.

Note that the result of text editing a selection cannot be a modification of the
surrounding context. Only the text within the selection is re-parsed and only the
selected subterm is changed.

Suppose, using the desk calculator of Appendix A, we were editing the object

Prod(Sum(Const(2),Const(3)),Const(4))

where the subterm Sum(Const(2),Const(3)) is the selection. Then the screen
would appear as

(⌈(2 + 3)⌉ * 4)

where the box is used to indicate the highlighted selection. Now suppose we
text edit the selection and delete the parentheses enclosing 2+3. Then just
before initiating the parse, the screen would appear as:

(⌈2 + 3⌉▌ * 4)

When a parse is triggered, say by the command **forward-with-optionals**, the
2+3 reparses as an expression and the computed replacement term is
Sum(Const(2),Const(3)), exactly what was there originally. The net effect is
that the expression is unchanged. When the object is redisplayed, the

parentheses reappear, because they are generated according to the term's unparsing schemes.

By contrast, suppose the selection were the entire expression:

$\boxed{((2 + 3) \ast 4)}$

and we delete the same parentheses. In this case, when the text string (2+3*4) is reparsed the * takes precedence over the + and the resulting change to the structure of the selection is reflected in the altered parenthesization of the term as displayed:

(2+(3*4))

3.6. Changing the Structural Selection by Traversal of the Edited Term

The selection of a buffer can be changed by advancing structurally through the abstract-syntax tree relative to the current selection, (*e.g.* in preorder, reverse preorder, by moving to the parent, *etc.*). If such a motion would cause the selection to leave the window, the object's position with respect to the window is automatically adjusted by scrolling. If the current selection is a placeholder for an optional constituent, that placeholder is removed in the course of advancing the selection beyond the optional term. Some commands never stop at placeholders for optional constituents, while others insert a placeholder at such places and stop there.

Not every node of the abstract-syntax tree is a legitimate location for the apex of the selection. Resting places are defined in the specification, as described in Section 2.6, "View and Unparsing Declarations."

forward-preorder   ^N
   Change the selection to the next resting place in a forward preorder traversal of the abstract-syntax tree. Do not stop at placeholders for optional constituents.

backward-preorder   ^P
   Change the selection to the previous resting place in a forward preorder traversal of the abstract-syntax tree. Do not stop at placeholders for optional constituents.

right   ^F
   If there is no text buffer, **right** is the same as **forward-preorder**. See Section 3.7 for the meaning of **right** when there is a text buffer.

left   ^B

If there is no text buffer, **left** is the same as **backward-preorder**. See Section 3.7 for the meaning of **left** when there is a text buffer.

forward-with-optionals   ^M

Change the selection to the next resting place in a forward preorder traversal of the abstract-syntax tree. Stop at placeholders for optional constituents. Note that the control character ^M is RETURN.

backward-with-optionals   ^H

Change the selection to the previous resting place in a forward preorder traversal of the abstract-syntax tree. Stop at placeholders for optional constituents.

forward-sibling   ESC-^N

Bypass all resting places contained within the current selection and advance to the next sibling in a forward preorder traversal of the abstract-syntax tree. If there is no next sibling, ascend to the enclosing resting place and advance to its next sibling, *etc.* Do not stop at placeholders for optional constituents.

backward-sibling   ESC-^P

Bypass all resting places contained within the current selection and advance to the previous sibling in a forward preorder traversal of the abstract-syntax tree. If there is no previous sibling, ascend to the enclosing resting place and advance to its previous sibling, *etc.* Do not stop at placeholders for optional constituents.

forward-sibling-with-optionals   ESC-^M

Same as **forward-sibling**, but stopping, in addition, at placeholders for optional constituents.

backward-sibling-with-optionals   ESC-^B

Same as **backward-sibling**, but stopping, in addition, at placeholders for optional constituents.

ascend-to-parent   ESC-\

Change the selection to the closest enclosing resting place.

beginning-of-file   ESC-<

Change the selection to the root of the abstract-syntax tree.

end-of-file   ESC->

Change the selection to the rightmost resting place in the abstract-syntax tree.

advance-after-parse

If textual entry is terminated by **forward-with-optionals**, then upon successful analysis the **forward-with-optionals** command is replaced by **advance-after-parse**. Let t be the subterm or sublist that has replaced the selection as a result of textual input. The **advance-after-parse** command advances to the first existing placeholder within t in a forward preorder traversal. Optional placeholders are never inserted within t by **advance-after-parse**. If no existing placeholder is contained in t, then the selection is changed to the first resting place beyond t in a forward preorder traversal. In locating such a resting place, **advance-after-parse** may insert optional placeholders after t.

advance-after-transform

If a transformation command is terminated by **forward-with-optionals**, then upon successful analysis the **forward-with-optionals** command is replaced by **advance-after-transform**. Let t be the result of applying a transformation to the current selection, as described in Section 2.8, "Transformation Declarations." The **advance-after-transform** command advances to the first existing placeholder within t, if there is one. If no existing placeholder is contained in t, the selection is left unchanged. Optional placeholders are never inserted within t by **advance-after-transform**.

forward-after-parse

If textual entry is terminated by **forward-preorder**, then upon successful analysis the **forward-preorder** command is replaced by **forward-after-parse**. Let t be the subterm or sublist that has replaced the selection as a result of textual input. If no existing placeholder occurs within t, then **forward-after-parse** stops at the first resting place beyond t. **Forward-after-parse** never inserts optional placeholders either in t or beyond t.

3.7. Changing the Character Selection by Traversal of the Text Buffer

As described in Section 3.5, text being entered or re-edited resides in a text buffer displayed, in place, within its enclosing structural context. One character within the text buffer is selected. This character selection can be redirected to another character within the text buffer by normal horizontal and vertical "cursor-motion" commands. Movement of the character selection beyond the boundaries of the text buffer causes the text to be submitted for analysis and translation. Within a text buffer, the structural-motion commands **forward-preorder**, **backward-preorder**, **right**, and **left** have been overloaded and move the character selection down, up, right, and left, respectively.

forward-preorder   ^N

Move the character selection one position down. If already at the last line of the text buffer, this command is interpreted as **forward-after-parse**, as described in Section 3.6, provided the text is syntactically correct.

backward-preorder   ˆP

Move the character selection one position up. If already at the first line of
the text buffer, this command is interpreted as **backward-preorder**, as
described in Section 3.6, provided the text is syntactically correct.

right   ˆF

Move the character selection one position to the right. If already at the
rightmost character of a line, the character selection advances to the first
character of the next line of the text buffer. If already at the rightmost character of the last line of the text buffer, the command is interpreted as
forward-after-parse.

left   ˆB

Move the character selection one position to the left. If already at the leftmost character of a line, the character selection advances to the last character of the previous line of the text buffer. If already at the leftmost character
of the first line of the text buffer, the command is interpreted as **backward-
preorder**.

beginning-of-line   ˆA

Move the character selection to the beginning of the line.

end-of-line   ˆE

Move the character selection to the end of the line.

3.8. Moving the Object With Respect to the Window

It is sometimes desirable to move the object with respect to the window without
changing the current selection. In editors generated for video-display terminals,
this is usually accomplished by issuing scrolling commands. In editors generated for workstations with bitmapped displays, it can also be accomplished by
clicking on the appropriate actuator of a scroll bar. See Appendix D, "Keyboards, Displays, Window Systems, and Mice" for additional details.

scroll-to-bottom

Scroll the object with respect to the window so that the last line of the object
appears in the middle of the window.

scroll-to-top

Scroll the object with respect to the window so that the first line of the object
appears on the first line of the window.

selection-to-top   ESC-!

Scroll the object with respect to the window so that the first line of the selection appears on the first line of the window.

next-page   ^V

Move the object up with respect to the window, effectively moving the view of the object down one page.

previous-page   ESC-v

Move the object down with respect to the window, effectively moving the view of the object up one page.

next-line   ^Z

Move the object up with respect to the window by one line, effectively moving the view of the object down one line.

previous-line   ESC-z

Move the object down with respect to the window by one line, effectively moving the view of the object up one line.

page-left   ESC-{

Move the object right with respect to the window, effectively moving the view of the object one page to the left.

page-right   ESC-}

Move the object left with respect to the window, effectively moving the view of the object one page to the right.

column-left

Move the object right with respect to the window, effectively moving the view of the object one column to the left. A column is one character wide. If a proportional font is in use, a column is the width of the character 0.

column-right

Move the object left with respect to the window, effectively moving the view of the object one column to the right.

3.9. Moving the Locator on the Screen

In editors generated for workstations equipped with a mouse, the mouse is used as a locator or pointer. Using the mouse, it is possible to point anywhere in the object pane, click a button, and change the current selection, as described in Section 3.10, "Changing the Selection with the Locator."

The commands described in this section work only in editors generated for video-display terminals, in which the terminal's cursor (*e.g.* highlighted box, underscore, *etc.*) is used as a locator, or poor man's mouse. It is important to bear in mind that the locator is distinct from the selection. The locator identifies a point on the screen and not a point in the buffer. If at all possible, the cursor keys of the terminal should be bound to the following commands.

pointer-left   ESC-b

Move the locator one character to the left. If already in column one of the object pane and not already at the leftmost scroll position, scroll the window.

pointer-right   ESC-f

Move the locator one character to the right. If already at the right border of the object pane, scroll the window.

pointer-up   ESC-p

Move the locator one character up. If already at the top of the object pane and not already at the uppermost scroll position, scroll the window.

pointer-down   ESC-d

Move the locator one character down. If already at the bottom of the object pane, scroll the window.

pointer-long-left

Move the locator eight characters to the left. If already within the first eight columns of the object pane and not already at the leftmost scroll position, scroll the window.

pointer-long-right

Move the locator eight characters to the right. If already within the right-most eight columns of the object pane, scroll the window.

pointer-long-up

Move the locator eight characters up. If already within the first eight rows of the object pane and not already at the leftmost scroll position, scroll the window.

pointer-long-down

Move the locator eight characters down. If already within the bottommost eight rows of the object pane, scroll the window.

pointer-top-of-screen   ESC-,

Move the locator to the first line of the screen.

pointer-bottom-of-screen   ESC-.

Move the locator to the last line of the screen.

3.10. Changing the Selection with the Locator

The selection can be changed using a mouse or other locating device.

Assume the locator is pointing at a given character c_1. Let p_1 be the production instance in the term whose unparsing scheme causes c_1 to be displayed. Then the command **select-start** changes the current selection to be the nearest resting place enclosing p_1 and begins the process of *dragging*. Suppose now, while dragging is in progress, the locator is moved to character c_2, where c_2 is displayed as a result of the unparsing scheme associated with production instance p_2 in the tree. Then, as a result of moving the locator to c_2, the selection becomes the least common ancestor of p_1 and p_2. The least common ancestor of two siblings in a list is considered to be the sublist containing both siblings and all siblings between them. **Select-stop** terminates execution of dragging.

Characters displayed as a result of a conditional unparsing rule in a list phylum's binary operator are an exception to the rules stated above. As described in Section 2.6.4, such characters are treated as list separators. Executing **select-start** while the locator is pointing at a list separator causes the selection to move to a placeholder that is inserted between the two list elements adjacent to the separator.

The rules stated above assume that the current selection is structural and not textual. Now suppose the opposite, *i.e.* either a textual insertion is in progress or an existing selection is being re-edited textually. In either case, a text buffer containing the text is displayed in place, within its structural context. Pointing the locator at any character within the text buffer and executing **select-start** changes the *character selection* to that character. Pointing the locator at any character outside of the text buffer and executing **select-start** performs the implied structural selection, provided the text in the text buffer can be successfully analyzed. If the text contains a syntax error, the selection modification is abandoned, an error message is printed, and the character selection is changed to the point of error.

In editors generated for workstations equipped with a mouse, selection commands are bound to a mouse button: **select-start** is bound to button-down and **select-stop** is bound to button-up. See Appendix D for further details.

In the absence of a mouse, buttons are simulated on the keyboard. We recommend one key-binding for **select** and another key-binding for **select-transition**. These keys should be conveniently located near the cursor keys used for changing the position of the locator.

Executing **select-start** while pointing the locator at the character c has one additional significance: it identifies c as the future character selection in the event that the given structural selection is textually re-edited.

select   ESC-@

    Select-start followed by **select-stop**.

select-start

    Change the selection to the production instance whose unparsing scheme caused the printing of the character pointed at by the locator and begin dragging.

select-stop

Terminate dragging.

select-transition   ESC-t

Toggle between **select-start** and **select-stop**.

extend   ESC-(

Extend-start followed by **extend-stop**.

extend-start

Let p_1 be the apex of the current selection, let c_2 be the character currently
pointed at by the locator, and let p_2 be the production instance whose
unparsing scheme caused the display of c_2. The effect of **extend-start** is to
change the selection to the least common ancestor of p_1 and p_2, and com-
mence dragging.

extend-stop

Stop dragging.

extend-transition   ESC-X

Toggle between **extend-start** and **extend-stop**.

3.11. Structural Editing

Structural modifications follow a cut-and-paste paradigm. Only whole, well-
formed substructures can be removed and inserted.

cut-to-clipped   ^W

Move the selection of the current buffer to buffer CLIPPED. The new
selection becomes a placeholder at the point from which the selection was
removed. The previous contents of CLIPPED are lost.

copy-to-clipped   ESC-^W

Copy the selection of the current buffer to buffer CLIPPED. The previous
contents of CLIPPED are lost.

paste-from-clipped   ^Y

Move the contents of buffer CLIPPED into the buffer at the current selection, which must be a placeholder. In CLIPPED, a placeholder term
replaces the previous contents.

copy-from-clipped   ESC-^Y

Copy the contents of buffer CLIPPED into the buffer at the current selection, which necessarily must be a placeholder. The contents of CLIPPED
are left unchanged.

copy-text-from-clipped   ESC-^T

Copy the contents of buffer CLIPPED, as text, into a text buffer at the current selection immediately preceding the character selection. The contents of CLIPPED are left unchanged.

delete-selection   ˆK

Move the selection of the current buffer to buffer DELETED. The selection becomes a placeholder. The previous contents of DELETED are lost.

3.12. Textual Editing

As described in Section 3.5, textual insertion and textual re-editing are permitted in some contexts.

If a textual insertion is permitted at a placeholder, one merely begins to type, whereupon the text of the placeholder disappears and the keystrokes are echoed in the text buffer, which is displayed in place on the screen.

If textual re-editing of an existing structure is desired and is permitted, one establishes the character selection at the desired place and begins either to type or to erase characters. If the current selection was established by tree traversal, as described in Section 3.6, the textual-insertion point is at the beginning of the selection. If the current selection was established by locator selection, as described in Section 3.10, then the textual-insertion point is in front of the character at which the locator pointed when the **select-start** was executed.

delete-next-character   ˆD

Delete the current character selection. If the character selection is at the end of a line in the text buffer (other than the last line), then the current line and the next line are joined into one line.

delete-previous-character   DEL

Delete the character to the left of the character selection. If the character selection is at the beginning of a line in the text buffer (other than the first line), then the current line and the previous line are joined into one line.

erase-to-end-of-line   ESC-d

Erase from the character selection to the end of the line, including the character selection.

erase-to-beginning-of-line   ESC-DEL

Erase from the beginning of the line to the character selection, not including the character selection.

delete-selection   ˆK

Delete the entire line.

new-line   ˆJ

Insert a new line in the text buffer. Note that the control character ˆJ is LINE-FEED.

text-capture

Capture the text of the current selection into a text buffer regardless of the editing mode of the production at the apex of the selection. If there is no entry declaration for the phylum of the current selection, then **text-capture** fails.

undo   ^X^U

Delete the text buffer, and restore the selection to its state before the text-capture.

3.13. Access to Computed Attributes

dump-on

Create a textfile buffer associated with the current buffer. Call this buffer the associated *dump buffer*. Display the dump buffer in a second window. As the selection is moved from place to place in the current buffer, a display of the attributes at the apex of its selection are maintained in the dump buffer. The attributes of nodes immediately below the apex that are not resting places are also displayed in the dump buffer.

dump-off

Turn off the dynamic updating of the dump buffer associated with the current buffer. Warning: merely deleting the window displaying the dump buffer does not turn off the maintenance of the dump buffer.

show-attribute *attribute-name buffer-name*

Copy the value of the named attribute of the current selection to the named buffer. The given buffer acquires the syntactic mode of the attribute.

write-attribute *attribute-name file-name*

Write the named attribute of the current selection to the named file in textual format.

3.14. Searching

search-forward *text phylum-name operator-name*   ESC-^F

Search forward from the current selection, in preorder, for the next occurrence of either a STR value equal to the given text, an instance of a term of the given phylum, or an instance of a term having the given operator. On reaching the end of the object, wrap around to the root and continue searching.

search-reverse *text phylum-name operator-name*   ESC-^R

Search backward from the current selection, in the reverse of a preorder traversal, for the next occurrence of either a STR value equal to the given text, an instance of a term of the given phylum, or an instance of a term with the given operator. On reaching the root of the object, wrap around to the rightmost leaf and continue searching.

3.15. Alternating Unparsing Schemes

As described in Section 2.6, "View and Unparsing Declarations," each production can have up to two unparsing schemes. These are termed the "principal" scheme and the "alternate" scheme. The alternate unparsing scheme is typically used for displaying a production in an abbreviated format. The commands below are used to switch between the principal and alternate unparsing schemes.

Which scheme is in use at a given production is preserved when an object is written to a file in structure format. Thus, upon re-reading such a file, the unparsing is unchanged. Note, however, that when an object is written to a file in text format, it is written exactly as it appears on the screen. Thus, if large sections of an object have been abbreviated (*e.g.* by . . .) they will be lost in the text file.

alternate-unparsing-off

Throughout the current buffer, all nodes are set to use the principal, rather than the alternate, unparsing scheme.

alternate-unparsing-on

Throughout the current buffer, all nodes that have alternate unparsing schemes are set to use the alternate scheme.

alternate-unparsing-toggle   ESC-e

Change the selection to the closest enclosing node that has an alternate unparsing scheme in the view associated with the current window and then toggle its current unparsing scheme. If the two unparsing schemes are used for unelided and elided displays, this has the effect of hiding and revealing substructures of the buffer.

CHAPTER 4

The SSL Debugger

The SSL debugger provides facilities for finding errors in editor specifications and for profiling editors.

To make an editor that includes the debugger, use the –debug flag of sgen when generating the editor. (Be aware that incorporation of the debugger in an editor degrades performance.)

An editor that has been generated with the –debug flag can be invoked with the –d flag, whereupon control will enter the debugger with the message

```
SSL Debugger
type 'h' for help
(debug)
```

Invoking such an editor without the –d flag causes the editor to begin execution normally. While an editor is running, executing the command **break-to-debugger** causes entry to the debugger upon the next execution of an SSL expression. In editors generated for video-display terminals, the command ˆC is equivalent to **break-to-debugger**.

The debugger is a symbolic debugger for the stack code generated for SSL expressions. Interaction with the debugger is through the UNIX standard input and output files. The following facilities are provided:

1) Breakpoints can be set at the entry and exit points of functions and attribute equations.

2) Single-step execution of the SSL byte-codes is provided.
3) The SSL stack containing function arguments and sub-expression values can be displayed.
4) The tokenization of input text during parsing can be traced (lexical tracing).

The debugger commands are as follows:

b *name*	set entry breakpoint
B *name*	set exit breakpoint
c	continue
C	clear profiling information
d *name*	delete entry breakpoint
D *name*	delete exit breakpoint
e	enable lexical tracing
E	disable lexical tracing
f	print active functions without their parameters
h	print help message
l	print next instruction
n	continue, but stop in the next call to the interpreter
p	print profiling information to file ssl_profile
P *name*	profile a particular function
q	quit editor
s	execute next step
t	print topmost active function and its parameters
T	same as t, plus stacked sub-expressions
w	print active functions and their parameters
W	same as w, plus stacked sub-expressions

In breakpoint commands, *name* can be either an SSL function name or an attribute reference of the form *phylum .attribute-name* or *operator .attribute-name*.

The user of the debugger should be aware of several optimizations performed on the SSL byte codes:

1) The evaluation of a boolean expression is short-circuited when enough of the expression has been evaluated to determine the value of the entire expression.
2) Because tail-recursive function invocations reuse the same activation record, only one activation record for a series of tail-recursive calls will appear on the stack. Furthermore, a single return instruction terminates the entire

series of tail-recursive calls.

3) When the i-th argument in a tail-recursive call is the i-th parameter of the function, the argument is not pushed on the stack.

4) At the beginning of execution, constant expressions are evaluated once and are saved in a constant pool. Thereafter, each constant expression is evaluated by fetching the value from the constant pool.

If an editor does a substantial amount of computation in attribute equations, the debugger's profiling capabilities may be useful. Often, a substantial fraction of the total execution time is spent in just a few functions, and with a little thought those functions can be made more efficient.

The first execution of the debugger command **p** activates profiling. Thereafter, each successive **p** command prints all accumulated profiling information to the file **ssl_profile**. The **C** command resets all accumulated profiling information. The debugger command **P** *name* indicates that profiling is to be performed only within the dynamic scope of the named function.

The profiler counts the number of times each SSL function is called and the number of interpreter op-codes that are executed in each function. For each function, the profiler only records the op-codes executed directly by that function; *i.e.* it does not include op-codes executed indirectly in functions called from that function. Note that the profiler lists the number of byte-codes executed and not the time spent in each function; the number of byte-codes executed can be taken as a rough approximation of the time spent executing the function.

The profiler also lists a count of the total number of executions of each byte-code.

CHAPTER 5

Interface to C

It is possible to combine a generated editor with code written directly in the C programming language. Because the Synthesizer Generator is implemented in C, such code can take advantage of all internal facilities of the implementation. Code written in C may serve as a bridge between the generated editor and an existing application package, perhaps one not written in C.

This section describes the interfacing facilities available in SSL. Because code written in C will depend on internal implementation details of the Synthesizer Generator, this section is, at best, only an introduction to the facilities and a sketch of how they may be used.

Section 5.1 describes how functions written in C can be called from SSL and *vice versa*. Section 5.2 explains how new SSL primitive types can be implemented in C. Section 5.3 describes a mechanism whereby attributes normally scattered throughout a tree can be stored and processed together. Section 5.4 illustrates how to define new commands.

As described in Appendix B, the shell program sgen can be passed C source files as arguments. All files with the extension .c are compiled using cc and are loaded together with the generated editor. C code can also be placed directly within an SSL source file wherever a declaration is permitted, using the following constructs:

```
%{
lines-of-C-declarations
%}
```

```
%[
lines-of-C-statements
%]
```

All C declarations appearing within %{ and %} braces and all C statements appearing within %[and %] brackets are concatenated and compiled together. Any C-preprocessor directives that are to be expanded as part of C compilation and not as part of SSL compilation should be escaped by a backslash preceding the hash mark.

5.1. Foreign and Exported Functions

A *foreign-function declaration* specifies the type of a C function that is callable from SSL. It has the form

$$phylum_0 \text{ \textbf{foreign} } function\text{-}name \text{ (}$$
$$phylum_1 \ parameter\text{-}name_1,$$
$$phylum_2 \ parameter\text{-}name_2,$$
$$\ldots ,$$
$$phylum_k \ parameter\text{-}name_k$$
$$\text{) ;}$$

A foreign function is called exactly as if the function had been written in SSL. A description of the C conventions needed for writing foreign functions is beyond the scope of this documentation, as they require knowledge of the internal structure of SSL terms. The interested reader is referred to the files **types.h** and **types.c** of the Synthesizer Generator source code, which contains the C implementations of foreign functions that implement the library functions for primitive phyla.

Foreign functions with a variable number of arguments are supported in a limited manner. The form

> $phylum_0$ **foreign** *function-name* (
> $phylum_1$ *parameter-name*$_1$,
> $phylum_2$ *parameter-name*$_2$,
> $\ldots$,
> $phylum_k$ *parameter-name*$_k$ **repeated**
>) ;

signifies that beyond the k-th argument, zero or more additional arguments are permitted, all of type $phylum_k$.

An *exported-function declaration* specifies that the given SSL function can be called from C functions, *e.g.* from foreign functions. Its form is

> $phylum_0$ **exported** *function-name* (
> $phylum_1$ *parameter-name*$_1$,
> $phylum_2$ *parameter-name*$_2$,
> $\ldots$,
> $phylum_k$ *parameter-name*$_k$
>) { *expression* } ;

The parameter and result types of exported and foreign functions can be parametric. See Section 2.11, "Quantified Declarations," for details and examples.

The keyword **exported** in a production declaration has the effect of exporting the definition of the operator for use in C code:

> *phylum-name* : **exported** *operator-name* ($phylum_1$ $phylum_2$ $\cdots$ $phylum_k$) ;

Specifying an operator to be exported causes a macro for the operator to be defined in the intermediate file **decls.h**. If **decls.h** is included at the start of a C source file, one can then use the operator to construct terms in the manner of SSL, *i.e.* in prefix notation.

5.2. Base-Type and Primitive-Phylum Definitions

New primitive phyla can be introduced. Definitions are given in two parts, a *base-type declaration* and a *primitive-phylum declaration.*

Base-type declarations

A base-type declaration defines a new underlying representation for values. Each base-type declaration consists of the name of a C type and the names of ten operations on the type:

```
typedef C-type-name base-type-name with (
    op-name, op-name, op-name, op-name, op-name,
    op-name, op-name, op-name, op-name, op-name
    ) ;
```

New base-type values are represented as values of type *C-type-name*. The ten base-type operations, in order, perform the following functions: (1) compare two values, (2) convert from ASCII, (3) convert to ASCII, (4) increment a reference count, (5) decrement a reference count, (6) generate a default value, (7) write a value to a file (first-pass processing), (8) write a value to a file (second-pass processing), (9) read a value from a file, and (10) return a pointer to a reference-count field. The ten operations and the type definition for *C-type-name* are written in C.

Example 5.2(a). The following declaration defines newtype, a new base type.

```
typedef NEWTYPE newtype with (
    compare,
    convert_from_ascii,
    convert_to_ascii,
    increment_rc,
    decrement_rc,
    default_value,
    file_pass1,
    file_pass2,
    file_read,
    ptr_to_rc
    );
```

A typedef for NEWTYPE, the representation type for newtype, must be provided in C, for example:

```
%{
/* Representation of base-type values. */
typedef struct _newtype {

    . . .
    } *NEWTYPE;
%}
```

The following schema indicate the parameter- and return-type conventions of the ten operations:

```
%[
/* Return Equal, LessThan, or GreaterThan relation between *a and *b. */
COMPARISON compare(a, b)
    NEWTYPE *a, *b;
    {
    if (. . .) return(Equal);
    else if (. . .) return(LessThan);
    else return(GreaterThan);
    }


/* Parse a given string s and return the corresponding base-type value. */
NEWTYPE convert_from_ascii(s)
    char *s;
    {
    NEWTYPE temp;
    temp = (NEWTYPE)malloc(sizeof(struct _newtype));
    . . .
    return(temp);
    }


/* Convert the given base-type value *t to a string and emit. */
PROCEDURE convert_to_ascii(f, dest, t)
    FILE *f;
    void (*dest)();
    NEWTYPE *t;
    {
    /* let the character array b be the string representation of t. */
    . . .
    (*dest)(f, b);
    }


/* Increment the reference count for *t (if necessary). */
PROCEDURE increment_rc(t)
    NEWTYPE *t;
    {
    . . .
    }
```

```
/* Decrement the reference count for *t (if necessary). */
PROCEDURE decrement_rc(t)
     NEWTYPE *t;
     {
     . . .
     }


/* Return an arbitrary base-type value to be used in a completing term. */
NEWTYPE default_value() {
     NEWTYPE temp;
     temp = (NEWTYPE)malloc(sizeof(struct _newtype));
     . . .
     return(temp);
     }


/* first pass processing to write value *p to a file. */
PROCEDURE file_pass1(p, stream)
     NEWTYPE *p;
     FILE *stream;
     {
     . . .
     }


/* Second pass processing to write value *p to a file. */
PROCEDURE file_pass2(p, stream)
     NEWTYPE *p;
     FILE *stream;
     {
     . . .
     }


/* Processing to read a value from a file into *p. */
PROCEDURE file_read(p, stream)
     NEWTYPE *p;
     FILE *stream;
     {
     . . .
     }


/* Return a pointer to the reference-count field of p. */
int *ptr_to_rc(p)
     NEWTYPE *p;
     {
     . . .
     }
%]
```

Primitive-phylum declarations

A primitive-phylum declaration defines a new class of SSL values by specifying the base type that implements the primitive phylum.

> *phylum* : *operator-name = base-type-name = ;*

The definitions presented in the previous example allow defining a new phylum **NEWPHYLUM** with the declaration:

NEWPHYLUM: NewPhylum = newtype = ;

Although the base-type declaration includes a convert-from-ascii operation, this operation is incorporated only into the generated editor, and is not incorporated into the SSL translator to recognize strings that denote the new phylum's constants. To create values of the new phylum, the editor designer must make use of foreign functions (see Section 5.1).

For further examples of base-type and primitive-phylum definitions, the reader is referred to the file **atoms.ssl**, the standard prefix that is prepended to all editor specifications, and to the files **types.h** and **types.c** of the Synthesizer Generator's implementation.

Primitive phyla can be parametric. See Section 2.11, "Quantified Declarations," for details and examples.

5.3. External Stores and External Computers

An *external store* is a table in which attributes can be maintained apart from the attributed tree. The external-store mechanism has several advantages and applications. First, it permits attribute values to be stored elsewhere — in a different process or even on different machines. Second, it permits related attributes that are scattered throughout the program tree to be grouped together. Third, it allows the communication of attributes to another module, for example, a graphics package or an inference engine.

The editor designer specifies that certain attributes will be maintained by an external store; the external store is then responsible for faithfully storing those values. An external store must provide operations to fetch an attribute's value, accept new values, and delete old values. The incremental attribute evaluator maintains the consistency of values in the store by sending delete and store messages whenever an externally stored attribute changes value. Values are retrieved from the store in response to fetch messages.

An *external computer* is just a routine that is invoked once per editing transaction. Invocation of the external computer provides the opportunity to process values in an external store periodically or to initiate some external event. The form of an external computer declaration is:

---

ext_computers *list-of-external-computer-names* ;

---

where an *external-computer-name* is the name of a procedure written in C.

External stores are defined statically, as part of the editor specification. A store declaration in SSL consists of the store name, a phylum for the kind of value to be placed in the store, and four *store-interface procedures* to initialize the store, to fetch values, insert new values, and delete old values, respectively:

---

store *store-name phylum* with
  (*initialize-routine-name,*
   fetch-routine-name,
   insert-routine-name,
   delete-routine-name
) ;

The four store routines are implemented as C procedures. The initialization routine of each declared external store is called once when the editor is first invoked.

An attribute declaration may include a list of external stores. Such attribute declarations have one of the following forms:

---

store (*list-of-stores*) synthesized *phylum attribute-name* ;
store (*list-of-stores*) inherited *phylum attribute-name* ;
store (*list-of-stores*) local *phylum attribute-name* ;
demand store (*list-of-stores*) synthesized *phylum attribute-name* ;
demand store (*list-of-stores*) inherited *phylum attribute-name* ;
demand store (*list-of-stores*) local *phylum attribute-name* ;

In a *list-of-stores*, the store name default_store refers to the normal storage mechanism for attributes, *i.e.* attached to the nodes of the term.

Let X be the nonterminal on the left-hand side of production instance p and let a be the i-th attribute of X. In each call to one of the store routines in connection with attribute instance $X.a$, the attribute instance is identified by two arguments: the address of p and the number i. Generated editors obey the following protocol:

1) Whenever $X.a$ receives a new value v, two procedure calls are made for each external store e named in a's declaration. First, the delete-routine of store e is called. Next, the insert-routine of store e is called.
2) Whenever the value of $X.a$ is needed, the fetch-routine of each external store e named in a's declaration is called.

Every external store e must observe the following rule: the value fetched for an attribute in e must be the value most recently inserted in e for that attribute. There are two exceptions to this rule. First, the special value NULLVALUE can be returned, in which case the attribute will be recomputed according to its defining attribute equation. Second, if the store is never listed first in a *list-of-stores*, then the value returned may be arbitrary because only the first store of an attribute is ever used to obtain the value.

Schema for an external store's interface procedures are as follows:

```
/* Initialize the store. */
initialize_routine_name()
        { . . . }

/* Delete attribute number a of production instance p. */
delete_routine_name(p,a)
    PROD_INSTANCE p;
    ATTR_NO a;
    { . . . }

/* Store v as the value of attribute number a of production instance p. */
insert_routine_name(p, a, v)
    PROD_INSTANCE p;
    ATTR_NO a;
    PROD_INSTANCE v;
    { . . . }

/* Fetch the stored value of attribute number a of production instance p. */
PROD_INSTANCE fetch_routine_name(p,a)
    PROD_INSTANCE p;
    ATTR_NO a;
    { . . . }
```

Because a store is implemented in C and must manipulate internal data structures of a generated editor, appropriate system include files will be required.

For an example of the use of external stores and computers, see the editor for the picture-drawing language *ideal* that is included with the Synthesizer Generator distribution.

5.4. Defining Additional Commands

Commands that produce side effects cannot be written in SSL; however, it is possible to write new commands using C, and have them linked into an editor when it is generated. This section first describes how to define commands that have no parameters; it then describes how to create *forms* for commands that do have parameters.

5.4.1. Defining commands that have no parameters

Defining a new command involves providing four pieces of information: the command's *name*, its *action*, its precedence with respect to the parsing of pending input text, and whether it is valid in a form.

1) A command's name is a string.
2) The command's action is a parameterless C procedure to carry out the appropriate activity.
3) There are two alternatives for specifying the relative precedence of parsing and command interpretation:

   CO_WITHOUT_PARSE
   CO_AFTER_PARSE

   The CO_WITHOUT_PARSE property means that executing the command will leave pending input text unchanged; the CO_AFTER_PARSE property means that the command will be executed only if pending input text parses successfully.
4) Some commands must not be executed within a pending parameter form. This property is specified by the two values

   CO_VALID_IN_FORM
   CO_INVALID_IN_FORM

The command module of the editor kernel is informed of the command's properties through the operation co_open(). This operation must be invoked for each command of the system; normally these calls are performed during editor initialization.

In the Generator's library, there is an initialization procedure init_sys3() that is normally a no-op. Because this procedure is loaded from a library, it may be redefined as the editor-designer sees fit; it should contain the calls on co_open() that define new commands.

In editors generated for mouse-based window systems, the newly defined command can be placed in one of the system command menus. The routine me_open() creates a new menu and the routine me_insert() enters a command into a given menu.

Below, we give a definition for the command **new-operation**, which does nothing. By including the file new_operation.c in the list of file arguments when sgen is invoked, this new command will be added to the generated editor.

```
/* File: new_operation.c */
# include "lang.h"
# include "commands.h"
# include "menu.h"

init_sys3() {
    ME me_user;
    extern PROCEDURE new_operation_command();
    co_open(
        "new-operation",
        new_operation_command,
        CO_WITHOUT_PARSE,
        CO_VALID_IN_FORM
        );
    me_user = me_open("User Commands");
    me_insert("new-operation", me_user);
    }

/* new-operation ----------------------------*/
PROCEDURE new_operation_command()
    {
    /* body of command here */
    }
```

5.4.2. Defining commands that have parameters

Commands that require parameters have an associated *form*. As soon as the command is initiated, the parameter form appears on the screen for the user to fill in values for the command's parameters. The form is a structured object, and parameters can be entered using the same editing operations that are used for any other buffer. After the parameters have been entered, the command is passed its parameters by executing **start-command**. A command can be canceled at any time during the editing of its parameters by executing **cancel-command**.

Let us now change the definition of the **new-operation** command so that it has two required parameters: an integer (INT) and a string (STR). The command will behave as follows:

1) If the INT parameter is 0, the message integer parameter is zero will be printed on the command line. In addition, the new-operation command will not complete; the form will remain on the screen and control will be returned to the user in a state where he may re-edit the form's parameters.

2) If the INT parameter is non-zero, the STR parameter will be printed on the command line. In this situation, the new-operation command will complete; the form will disappear from the screen, and the user will be back editing the object contained in the window from which the command was invoked.

3) Each time the command is invoked, the form will be initialized with an integer parameter of 10 and a placeholder for the string parameter.

The structure of the form is given by an SSL phylum definition for newForm:

```
/* Form for parameters of the new-operation command. */
newForm: NewForm( _number textline )
            [ ^: "NEW OPERATION   number: " @  " string: " @  ];
```

When the user executes the **new-operation** command, the initial form is created by the exported SSL function CreateNewForm. In general, CreateNewForm may have whatever parameters are needed; in the example below, one integer parameter is expected:

```
/* called by MakeNewForm to create the form value */
newForm exported CreateNewForm( INT i ){
  NewForm( _Number(INTtoNUMB(i)), [textline] )
  };
```

After the form has been edited, the user executes **start-command** to process the form. The processing is performed by the exported SSL function NewOperation. NewOperation returns a 1 to signal an error, 0 for success. (FAILURE and SUCCESS are defined constants equal to 1 and 0, respectively.)

```
INT foreign do_new_operation(INT i, STR s);
INT exported NewOperation(newForm f) {
  with(f)(
    NewForm(*, TextLineNil): 1,
    NewForm(_NumberBot, *): 1,
    NewForm(_Number(i), TextLine(str)):
      do_new_operation(STRtoINT(i), str)
    )
  };
```

NewOperation calls the foreign C function do_new_operation to actually perform the operation. The C routine do_new_operation returns 1 to signal error,
0 for success:

```
/* called when the start-command is issued */
FOREIGN do_new_operation(N, S)
   PROD_INSTANCE N;    /* an SSL INT */
   PROD_INSTANCE S;    /* an SSL STR */
   {
   int n;                   /* value of N */
   STRING st;               /* value of S as a char * */
   int answer;
   /* conversion of parameter values from SSL values to C values */
         n = IntValue(N);
         st = str0_to_str(StrValue(S));
   /* body of command here */
         if ( n == 0) {
            write_error_string( "integer parameter is zero" );
            answer = FAILURE;
            }
         else {
            write_msg( "second parameter was %s", st );
            answer = SUCCESS;
            }
   return( Int(answer) );
   }
```

The association of the command name with its action, its precedence with
respect to parsing, and its form behavior are handled in the same way as in the
case of commands without parameters; namely, init_sys3() calls co_open().
Note, however, that for commands with parameters, the procedure
new_operation_command calls the procedure execute_form_command.
The latter handles initializing the form and displaying it on the screen, where it
remains until the user either performs **start-command** or **cancel-command**.

```
# include "lang.h"
# include "structures.h"
# include "types.h"
# include "commands.h"
# include "buffers_exp.h"
# include "str0.h"

init_sys3() {
  ME me_user;
  extern PROCEDURE new_operation_command();
  co_open(
    "new-operation",
    new_operation_command,
    CO_WITHOUT_PARSE,
    CO_VALID_IN_FORM
    );
  me_user = me_open("User Commands");
  me_insert("new-operation", me_user);
  }


/* new-operation ----------------------------*/
PROCEDURE new_operation_command()
    {
  extern PROD_INSTANCE NewOperation();
  extern PROD_INSTANCE MakeNewForm();
  return (
        execute_form_command(
          "newForm",              /* phylum of form */
          "New Command  Form",   /* name of buffer for the form */
          1,                      /* height of displayed form */
          0,                      /* height of help pane of form */
          NewOperation,           /* SSL procedure to process form */
          MakeNewForm             /* form initialization routine, or NULL */
          )
        );
    }


/* called by execute_form_command to reinitialize the form */
static PROD_INSTANCE MakeNewForm(old_form, buf)
  PROD_INSTANCE old_form;  /* old value of the form */
  BUFFER buf;                      /* currently edited buffer */
  {
  extern PROD_INSTANCE CreateNewForm();
  return(CreateNewForm( Int(10) ));
  }
```

APPENDIX A

A Sample Specification

This appendix contains a complete specification of a simple desk calculator. The desk calculator allows one to create and modify a list of integer expressions, during which time each expression's value is incrementally computed and displayed.

The operations permitted are integer addition, subtraction, multiplication, and division. Each expression is displayed fully parenthesized. If a divisor is 0, an error message is printed and the value of the quotient is taken to be the value of the dividend. For example, a possible screen image of the generated editor is

```
┌─────────────────────────────────────────────────────────────┐
│┌─────────────────────────────────────────────────────────────┐│
││main                                                           ││
│└─────────────────────────────────────────────────────────────┘│
│                                                                │
│┌───────┐                                                       │
││<exp>  │                                                       │
│└───────┘                                                       │
│VALUE = 0;                                                      │
│                                                                │
│(2 /<—DIVISION BY ZERO—>(7 – 7))                                │
│VALUE = 2;                                                      │
│Positioned at calc   +   –   *   /   evaluate   let             │
└─────────────────────────────────────────────────────────────┘
```

In addition to the four arithmetic operations, a binding construct is provided that allows identifiers to be bound locally to values. This construct has the form

let <*name*> = <*exp₁*> in
 <*exp₂*>
ni

The value of the let construct is defined to be the value of <*exp₂*>, as computed
in an environment in which the given <*name*> is bound to the value of <*exp₁*>.
In computing <*exp₁*>, the given <*name*> is either unbound or has the value
defined in an enclosing let construct. If an unbound name occurs in an expression, the error message <—UNDEFINED is printed after the name and the
value of the name is taken to be 0. In the following example, in the expression
((a + b) + c), identifiers a, b, and c have values 2, 3, and 0, respectively.

let a = 1 in
 let b = (2 + a) in
  let a = (a + a) in
   ((a + b) + c<—UNDEFINED)
  ni
 ni
ni
VALUE = 5

Expressions and subexpressions can be entered either textually or by template
insertion. The commands +, −, *, /, and let insert templates for the corresponding constructs. In textual input, parentheses are optional and * and / take precedence over + and −. Commands for transforming expressions according to the
distributive and commutative laws of arithmetic are provided, as is a command
to replace an expression with its value.

Fragments of this specification are used throughout the reference manual to
illustrate features of SSL. Line numbers appear within comment delimiters for
reference. The specification is written in three parts: lines 1 through 80 define a
bare-bones, four-function calculator; lines 81 through 169, define the let construct; lines 108A-154A, if inserted in lieu of lines 108-154, use the built-in
parametric phylum MAP[α,β] for the environments of name/value bindings.
(Lines 109-127 and 141-143 have no analogue in the alternative version.)

```
/*  1 */    /***********************************
/*  2 */     *  Desk-calculator specification  *
/*  3 */     ***********************************/
/*  4 */
/*  5 */    /* Abstract syntax */
/*  6 */    root calc;
/*  7 */    list calc;
/*  8 */    calc: CalcNil()
/*  9 */       | CalcPair(exp calc)
/* 10 */       ;
/* 11 */    exp:  Null()
/* 12 */       | Sum, Diff, Prod, Quot(exp  exp)
/* 13 */       | Const(INT)
/* 14 */       ;
/* 15 */
/* 16 */    /* Attribution rules for expression evaluation */
/* 17 */    exp {synthesized INT v; };
/* 18 */    exp:  Null { exp.v = 0; }
/* 19 */       | Sum   { exp$1.v = exp$2.v + exp$3.v; }
/* 20 */       | Diff    { exp$1.v = exp$2.v – exp$3.v; }
/* 21 */       | Prod  { exp$1.v = exp$2.v * exp$3.v; }
/* 22 */       | Quot  { local STR error;
/* 23 */          error = (exp$3.v==0) ? "<—DIVISION BY ZERO—>" : "";
/* 24 */          exp$1.v = (exp$3.v==0) ? exp$2.v : (exp$2.v / exp$3.v) ;
/* 25 */          }
/* 26 */       | Const{ exp$1.v = INT; }
/* 27 */       ;
/* 28 */
/* 29 */    /* Unparsing */
/* 30 */    calc: CalcPair[ @ ::= @ "%nVALUE = " exp.v [";%n%n"] @ ];
/* 31 */    exp: Null [ @ ::= "<exp>" ]
/* 32 */       | Sum  [ @ ::= "(" @ " + " @ ")" ]
/* 33 */       | Diff   [ @ ::= "(" @ " – " @ ")" ]
/* 34 */       | Prod  [ @ ::= "(" @ " * " @ ")" ]
/* 35 */       | Quot  [ @ ::= "(" @ " / " error @ ")" ]
/* 36 */       | Const[ @ ::= ^ ]
/* 37 */       ;
/* 38 */
```

```
/* 39 */     /* Template commands */
/* 40 */     transform exp on "+" <exp> : Sum ( <exp>, <exp> ),
/* 41 */                on "–" <exp> : Diff ( <exp>, <exp> ),
/* 42 */                on "*" <exp> : Prod ( <exp>, <exp> ),
/* 43 */                on "/" <exp> : Quot ( <exp>, <exp> )
/* 44 */                ;
/* 45 */
/* 46 */     /* Lexical syntax */
/* 47 */     INTEGER: < [0–9]+ >;
/* 48 */     WHITESPACE: < [\ \t\n] >;
/* 49 */
/* 50 */     /* Parse syntax */
/* 51 */     Calc { synthesized calc abs; };
/* 52 */     Exp  { synthesized exp abs; };
/* 53 */
/* 54 */     left '+', '–';
/* 55 */     left '*', '/';
/* 56 */
/* 57 */     Calc::= (Exp)    { Calc.abs  = CalcPair(Exp.abs, CalcNil()); }
/* 58 */         | (Exp  Calc) { Calc$1.abs = CalcPair(Exp.abs, Calc$2.abs); }
/* 59 */         ;
/* 60 */     Exp::= (INTEGER)  { $$.abs = Const(STRtoINT(INTEGER)); }
/* 61 */         | (Exp '+' Exp)   { $$.abs = Sum( Exp$2.abs, Exp$3.abs); }
/* 62 */         | (Exp '–' Exp)   { $$.abs = Diff(Exp$2.abs, Exp$3.abs); }
/* 63 */         | (Exp '*' Exp)   { $$.abs = Prod(Exp$2.abs, Exp$3.abs); }
/* 64 */         | (Exp '/' Exp)   { $$.abs = Quot(Exp$2.abs, Exp$3.abs); }
/* 65 */         | ('(' Exp ')')   { $$.abs = Exp$2.abs; }
/* 66 */         ;
/* 67 */
/* 68 */     calc ~ Calc.abs;
/* 69 */     exp  ~ Exp.abs;
/* 70 */
/* 71 */     /* Transformations */
/* 72 */     transform exp
/* 73 */        on "factor-left" Sum(Prod(a,b),Prod(a,c)): Prod(a,Sum(b,c)),
/* 74 */        on "factor-right" Sum(Prod(b,a),Prod(c,a)): Prod(Sum(b,c),a),
/* 75 */        on "distribute-left" Prod(a,Sum(b,c)): Sum(Prod(a,b),Prod(a,c)),
/* 76 */        on "distribute-right" Prod(Sum(b,c),a): Sum(Prod(b,a),Prod(c,a)),
/* 77 */        on "commute" Sum(a,b): Sum(b,a),
/* 78 */        on "commute" Prod(a,b): Prod(b,a),
/* 79 */        on "evaluate" t : Const(t.v)
/* 80 */        ;
```

```
/* 81 */    /************************************
/* 82 */     * Let-expression specification  *
/* 83 */    *************************************/
/* 84 */
/* 85 */    /* Abstract syntax */
/* 86 */    exp: Let( symb exp exp )
/* 87 */      | Use( ID )
/* 88 */      ;
/* 89 */    symb: DefBot( )
/* 90 */      | Dcf( ID )
/* 91 */      ;
/* 92 */
/* 93 */    /* Lexical syntax */
/* 94 */    LET: < "let" >;
/* 95 */    IN: < "in" >;
/* 96 */    NI: < "ni" >;
/* 97 */    ID: < [a–zA–Z][a–zA–Z0–9]* >;
/* 98 */
/* 99 */    /* Parse syntax */
/* 100 */    Symb { synthesized symb abs; };
/* 101 */    Exp::= (LET Symb '=' Exp IN Exp NI)
/* 102 */        { Exp$1.abs = Let( Symb.abs, Exp$2.abs, Exp$3.abs ); }
/* 103 */      | (ID) { Exp$1.abs = Use(ID); }
/* 104 */      ;
/* 105 */    Symb ::= (ID) { Symb.abs = Def(ID); };
/* 106 */    symb ~ Symb.abs;
/* 107 */
/* 108 */    /* Type definition for environments */
/* 109 */    list ENV;
/* 110 */    ENV: NullEnv( ) [ @: ]
/* 111 */      | EnvConcat( BINDING ENV ) [ @ : @ [",%n"] @ ]
/* 112 */      ;
/* 113 */    BINDING: Binding( ID INT ) [ @ : @ "=" @ ];
/* 114 */
```

```
/* 115 */    /*
/* 116 */     *  lookup(id,env)
/* 117 */     *
/* 118 */     *  Return first Binding(s,*) in env such that id==s,
/* 119 */     *  or Binding("?",0) if no such Binding exists.
/* 120 */     */
/* 121 */    BINDING lookup(ID id, ENV env) {
/* 122 */       with (env) (
/* 123 */          NullEnv: Binding("?", 0),
/* 124 */          EnvConcat(b, e):
/* 125 */             with (b) (Binding(s, *): ( id==s ? b : lookup(id, e)))
/* 126 */          )
/* 127 */       };
/* 128 */
/* 129 */    /* Attribute declarations */
/* 130 */    exp  { inherited ENV env; };
/* 131 */    symb { synthesized ID id; };
/* 132 */
/* 133 */    /* Attribution of abstract syntax */
/* 134 */    calc: CalcPair { exp.env = NullEnv; } ;
/* 135 */    exp: Let {
/* 136 */        exp$2.env = exp$1.env;
/* 137 */        exp$3.env = Binding(symb.id, exp$2.v) :: exp$1.env;
/* 138 */        exp$1.v = exp$3.v;
/* 139 */        }
/* 140 */      | Use {
/* 141 */        local BINDING b;
/* 142 */        local STR error;
/* 143 */        b = lookup( ID, exp.env);
/* 144 */        error = with(b)(Binding(s,*): s=="?" ? "<—UNDEFINED" : "");
/* 145 */        exp.v = with(b)(Binding(*,i): i);
/* 146 */        }
/* 147 */      | Sum, Diff, Prod, Quot {
/* 148 */        exp$2.env = exp$1.env;
/* 149 */        exp$3.env = exp$1.env;
/* 150 */        }
/* 151 */        ;
/* 152 */    symb: DefBot { symb.id = "?"; }
/* 153 */       |  Def { symb.id = ID; }
/* 154 */        ;
/* 155 */
```

```
/* 156 */      /* Unparsing */
/* 157 */      exp: Let [ @ :  "let %t" @  " = " @  " in%n" @  "%b%nni" ]
/* 158 */        | Use [ @ ::=  ^ error ]
/* 159 */        ;
/* 160 */      symb: DefBot [ @ ::=  "<name>" ]
/* 161 */        | Def [ @ ::=  ^ ]
/* 162 */        ;
/* 163 */
/* 164 */      /* Alternate unparsing declaration for let-expressions */
/* 165 */      exp: Let [ @ :  "let %t" @  " = <" .. exp$2.v "> in%n" @  "%b%nni" ];
/* 166 */
/* 167 */      /* Template command */
/* 168 */      transform exp on "let" <exp>: Let( <symb>, <exp>, <exp> );
/* 169 */


/* 108A */     /* Implementation of environments using MAP attributes */
/* 128A */
/* 129A */     /* Attribute declarations */
/* 130A */     exp  { inherited MAP[ID,INT] env; };
/* 131A */     symb { synthesized ID id; };
/* 132A */
/* 133A */     /* Attribution of abstract syntax */
/* 134A */     calc: CalcPair { exp.env = [ID |-> 0]; } ;
/* 135A */     exp: Let {
/* 136A */         exp$2.env = exp$1.env;
/* 137A */         exp$3.env = exp$1.env [symb.id |-> exp$2.v];
/* 138A */         exp$1.v = exp$3.v;
/* 139A */         }
/* 140A */       | Use {
/* 144A */         error = (ID in exp.env) ? "<--UNDEFINED" : "";
/* 145A */         exp.v = exp.env(ID);
/* 146A */         }
/* 147A */       | Sum, Diff, Prod, Quot {
/* 148A */         exp$2.env = exp$1.env;
/* 149A */         exp$3.env = exp$1.env;
/* 150A */         }
/* 151A */        ;
/* 152A */     symb: DefBot { symb.id = "?"; }
/* 153A */        | Def { symb.id = ID; }
/* 154A */        ;
```

APPENDIX B

Invoking the Synthesizer Generator

NAME

> sgen – Synthesizer Generator

SYNOPSIS

> sgen [option] ... file ...

DESCRIPTION

> Sgen is a system for generating a language-based editor from a language specification. Editor specifications are written in the Synthesizer Specification Language (SSL). Arguments to sgen whose names end with .ssl are taken to be SSL source files. Arguments to sgen whose names end with .c (.o) are taken to be C source (object) files. They are compiled and linked into the generated editor. Other arguments are ignored. In the absence of the −o flag, the generated editor is called syn.out.
>
> To use sgen, the location of a directory containing the Synthesizer Generator must be specified. This can be done in one of two ways: either as the value of environment variable SYNLOC or as the contents of file /usr/local/lib/synloc. This location is referred to below as SYNLOC. The default system location is SYNLOC/sys.
>
> Options to sgen include:

−a *alt_directory*

> Search for files in directory *alt_directory* if they are not found in the current directory. Multiple −a options are allowed.

-b

Use the COLLECTIONS implementation of maps instead of the AVL-tree implementation. Available only with the ATO attribute-evaluation kernel. (See the –kernel flag.)

-d

Make all attributes demand attributes.

-dbx

Invoke dbx on the SSL language processor. So that dbx can run ssl with the proper arguments, an appropriate run command is placed in a file named .rundbx. This command may be invoked by giving the dbx command: source .rundbx.

-debug

Use a version of the SSL interpreter that includes the SSL debugger.

-D *name*

Define *name* for the macro preprocessor. The .ssl source files are processed by the macro preprocessor, as are the lex file lex.yy.c, the yacc file y.tab.c, the generated grammar tables, and any *.c files specified as arguments to sgen.

-g

Pass the –g flag to the C compiler. By default, either the –g flag or the –O flag is passed to the C compiler. This default is installation specific.

-G

Provide diagnostic output about the plans that are generated by the ORDERED evaluation strategy. This output is only provided if the –kernel ORDERED option is specified.

-I *name*

Append *name* to the macro preprocessor's search path.

-kernel *kernel*

Use an alternative attribute-evaluation strategy. Allowable values are UNORDERED, ORDERED, and ATO; the default value is ORDERED.

The UNORDERED kernel implements Reps's original algorithm for incremental attribute evaluation. It works for any noncircular attribute grammar but has a somewhat high time and space overhead.

The ORDERED kernel incorporates an incremental version of Kastens's algorithm for attribute evaluation. It is more efficient than the UNORDERED kernel but works only for the ordered subclass of attribute grammars.

The ATO kernel incorporates Hoover's attribute-updating algorithm based on approximate topological ordering. It works for any noncircular attribute grammar and provides an optional implementation of MAP-valued attributes that is particularly efficient (see the −b flag). Although the ATO evaluator works well in practice, it does not have the optimal worst-case behavior of the other kernels.

−K

Test the grammar for circularity.

−I

Do not remove generated intermediate files.

−L *lexdecls*

When sgen invokes lex, prepend declarations from the file *lexdecls*.

−n

Provide warnings about attribute equations that are not in normal form.

−o *output*

Name the generated editor *output* instead of syn.out.

−O

Pass the −O flag to the C compiler. By default, either the −g flag or the −O flag is passed to the C compiler. This default is installation specific.

−pg

Create an editor that does profiling.

−r

If possible, avoid making unnecessary calls on yacc, lex, and cc. Sgen compares the newly generated intermediate files with any previously generated intermediate files in the directory. If certain files are identical, some of the steps of generating an editor are skipped. The new intermediate files are retained for future comparisons.

−s *sysloc*

> Use the substitute version of the system from directory SYNLOC/*sysloc*.

−saveas

> Save the pseudocode input file as pseudo.s. This file may be helpful while debugging a specification.

−savessl

> Save the input to ssl in file Savessl. This file may be helpful while debugging a specification.

−S *sysloc*

> Use a substitute version of the system from directory *sysloc* instead of SYNLOC/sys.

−v

> Invoke yacc with the −v flag, so that diagnostic file y.output will be produced.

−w *window_type*

> Create an editor for a *window_type* window system. Allowable values for *window_type* are VIDEO, SUN, X10, X11 and X. The default is installation specific. *Window_type* X denotes the latest supported version of the X Window System.

The following options are useful primarily for debugging different parts of the system.

−interp *interp*

> Use the alternative interpreter found in directory SYSLOC/obj/INTERP/*interp*. (See also the −debug option.)

−lang *lang*

> Use an alternative version of the SSL compiler from directory *lang*.

−lib *lib*

> Use the alternative library module found in directory SYSLOC/obj/LIB/*lib*.

−window *window*

> Use the alternative window system found in directory SYSLOC/obj/WINDOW/*window*.

−T *testloc*

> Search the directory structure rooted at *testloc* for parts of the system. Any object module found in *testloc* will be used instead of the system copy.

Unrecognized options are passed to the SSL compiler.

AUTHOR

Thomas Reps and Tim Teitelbaum.

FILES

file.ssl	input file
syn.out	editor created by sgen
sysloc	SYNLOC/sys or location given with −S or −s flag
sysloc/atoms.ssl	standard SSL prefix, including definitions of atomic types
sysloc/obj/INTERP	SSL interpreters needed by an editor
sysloc/obj/KERNEL	editor kernels for the various evaluation schemes
sysloc/obj/LANG/SSL/ssl	SSL language processor
sysloc/obj/LIB	library files needed by an editor
sysloc/obj/WINDOW	window system needed by an editor
sysloc/include/*	include files needed for compilation
sysloc/eval.c	file into which grammar tables are included and then compiled

SEE ALSO

Reps, T. and Teitelbaum, T. *The Synthesizer Generator Reference Manual*, Springer-Verlag, New York, NY (Third Edition: 1988).

Reps, T. and Teitelbaum, T. *The Synthesizer Generator: A System for Constructing Language-Based Editors*, Springer-Verlag, New York, NY (1988).

yacc (1), lex (1), cc (1), dbx (1), gprof (1)

BUGS

Because intermediate-file names are fixed, at most one sgen process can be active in a given directory at a time.

APPENDIX C
List of Editor Commands

advance-after-parse	
advance-after-transform	
alternate-unparsing-off	
alternate-unparsing-on	
alternate-unparsing-toggle	ESC-e
apropos	ESC-?
ascend-to-parent	ESC-\
backward-preorder	^P
backward-sibling	ESC-^P
backward-sibling-with-optionals	ESC-^B
backward-with-optionals	^H
beginning-of-file	ESC-<
beginning-of-line	^A
break-to-debugger	
cancel-command	ESC-c
column-left	
column-right	
copy-from-clipped	ESC-^Y
copy-text-from-clipped	^T
copy-to-clipped	ESC-^W
cut-to-clipped	^W
delete-next-character	^D
delete-other-windows	^X1
delete-previous-character	DEL

delete-selection	^K
delete-window	^Xd
dump-off	
dump-on	
end-of-file	ESC->
end-of-line	^E
enlarge-help	ESC-^Xz
enlarge-window	^Xz
erase-to-beginning-of-line	ESC-DEL
erase-to-end-of-line	ESC-d
execute-command	^I, ESC-x
execute-monitor-command	^X!
exit	^C, ESC-^C, ^X^C
extend	ESC-(
extend-start	
extend-stop	
extend-transition	ESC-X
forward-after-parse	
forward-preorder	^N
forward-sibling	ESC-^N
forward-sibling-with-optionals	ESC-^M
forward-with-optionals	^M
help-off	
help-on	
illegal-operation	^G, ESC-^G, ^X^G
insert-file	^X^I
left	^B
list-buffers	^X^B
new-buffer	
new-line	^J
next-line	^Z
next-page	^V
next-window	^Xn
page-left	ESC-{
page-right	ESC-}
paste-from-clipped	^Y
pointer-bottom-of-screen	ESC-.
pointer-down	ESC-d
pointer-left	ESC-b
pointer-long-down	

pointer-long-left	
pointer-long-right	
pointer-long-up	
pointer-right	ESC-f
pointer-top-of-screen	ESC-,
pointer-up	ESC-p
previous-line	ESC-z
previous-page	ESC-v
previous-window	^Xp
read-file	^X^F, ^X^R
redraw-display	^L
repeat-command	ESC-r
return-to-monitor	^_
right	^F
scroll-to-bottom	
scroll-to-top	
search-forward	ESC-^F
search-reverse	ESC-^R
select	ESC-@
select-start	
select-stop	
select-transition	ESC-t
selection-to-left	
selection-to-top	ESC-!
set-parameters	
show-attribute	
shrink-help	ESC-^X^Z
shrink-window	^X^Z
split-current-window	^X2
start-command	ESC-s
switch-to-buffer	^Xb
text-capture	
undo	^X^U
visit-file	^X^V
write-attribute	
write-current-file	^Xs
write-file-exit	^Xf
write-modified-files	^X^M
write-named-file	^X^W
write-selection-to-file	

APPENDIX D

Keyboards, Displays, Window Systems, and Mice

Editors may be generated for many different workstations, each with their own sort of keyboard and display screen. This appendix describes information that must be available to a running editor to describe the specific keyboard, display screen, and window system in use.

D.1. Keyboards

Key-bindings for commands are specified in a *keyboard description file*. Each command can have zero or more bindings. Each binding is defined on a separate line in the format

command-name one-or-more-octal-constants 000

A line in the format

command-name 000

signifies no key-binding. Each key-binding must be unique and no binding should be a prefix of any other. The lines of a keyboard description file must appear in lexicographic order of key-bindings. File syn_keyboard, containing the default bindings published in *The Synthesizer Generator Reference Manual*, is distributed with the system.

   Program change is provided to facilitate making a new keyboard description file from an old one, say from syn_keyboard. It eliminates the need to know the ASCII sequences generated by a terminal's programmable-function keys, cursor keys, *etc.* The program is located in an installation-specific location and is self-documenting.

A generated editor uses the value of variable SYNKBD of the UNIX environment to know the name of the keyboard description file. If SYNKBD is not defined, the value of variable TERM of the UNIX environment is used. When an editor is executed, a file with this name (optionally preceded by a period) is sought, first in the current working directory, next in the user's home directory, and finally in an installation-specific default directory. If no such file can be found, the same path is searched for a file named syn_keyboard or .syn_keyboard. Typically, the installation-specific default directory contains syn_keyboard.

The exact mechanism used to determine the installation-specific default directory containing keyboard-description files is the following. The directory is named keyboard, and the full path name of its parent directory is contained in file /usr/local/lib/synloc. This file would normally have been created by the system administrator at the time the Synthesizer Generator or the specific language-based editor was installed on the machine. Users wishing to override the default directory with their own can set the environment variable SYNLOC to be the full path name of the directory containing their own version of the keyboard directory. Thus, if the value of SYNLOC is p and the value of SYNKBD is t, the keyboard-description file sought is p/keyboard/t.

D.2. Displays and Window Systems

Each editor is generated for a specific window system using flag −w *window-type* of sgen. Allowable values for *window-type* are VIDEO, SUN, X10, X11 and X. X denotes the latest supported version of the X Window System, currently X11. The default window system selected by sgen in the absence of a −w flag is installation specific.

An editor generated with −w VIDEO will run on any video display terminal that is described in the UNIX termcap database. The termcap entry is chosen based on the value of variable TERM of the UNIX environment. An editor generated for video terminals will run in a terminal emulation window of the Sun-View or X window systems, albeit without supporting mouse-based selection and pop-up menus.

An editor generated for the SunView window system (*i.e.* with −w SUN) can be invoked only from within SunView. The font used by the editor can be selected by setting variable DEFAULT_FONT of the UNIX environment.

An editor generated for the X10 Window System must be invoked after an X10 window manager has been initiated. Editors generated for X10 support the standard X10 geometry and display specifications on the command line. In addition, a number of window properties can be defined in a ˜/.Xdefaults resource file. These window properties are:

Resource Name	Setting
Syn.Foreground	*color*
Syn.Background	*color*
Syn.BodyFont	*fontname*
Syn.PaneFont	*fontname*
Syn.SelectionFont	*fontname*

Syn.Foreground and Syn.Background are the colors of the foreground and background of window elements; the defaults are black and white, respectively. The usage of the various fonts is as follows:

- Syn.BodyFont for text within windows,
- Syn.PaneFont for menu titles, and
- Syn.SelectionFont for menu items.

An editor generated for the X11 Window System must be invoked after an X11 window manager has been initiated. Editors that have been compiled for the X11 window system accept the standard X11 –geometry and –display options on the command line. In addition, a number of window properties can be set on the command line of a running editor, in a ˜/.Xdefaults resource file, and in an XENVIRONMENT resource file. In the event of conflicting settings, the command line has highest priority and the ˜/.Xdefaults file has lowest priority. These window properties and their respective command-line flags and resource names are:

Command flag	Resource Name	Setting
–foreground	Syn.Foreground	*color*
–background	Syn.Background	*color*
–lf	Syn.Browser.Label.Font	*fontname*
–mf	Syn.Browser.Menu.Font	*fontname*
–cf	Syn.Browser.Command.Font	*fontname*
–of	Syn.Browser.Object.Font	*fontname*

Syn.Foreground and Syn.Background are the colors of the foreground and background of window elements; the defaults are black and white, respectively. The usage of the various fonts is as follows:

- Syn.Browser.Label.Font for window titles,
- Syn.Browser.Menu.Font for pop-up menus,
- Syn.Browser.Command.Font for the help-pane buttons, and
- Syn.Browser.Object.Font for the object pane.

Editors making use of multiple fonts and font characteristics require a style-definition file, whose location is given by variable SYNSTYLE of the UNIX environment. The form of a style-definition file is described in Section 2.6.

D.3. Mice

Editors generated for either the X Window System or SunView can make use of a mouse, while editors generated for video displays cannot. Editors generated for X10 and SunView make use of three buttons. On some workstations, the middle button is simulated by chording both buttons.

The leftmost button has the following uses:

- The selection in the object pane can be changed by clicking or dragging across non-blank characters in the display of an object.
- A transformation can be invoked by clicking on the transformation's name in a help pane.
- The display of an object can be scrolled within the window by clicking on one of the arrows in a scroll bar.

The middle button is used to control a pop-up menu containing language-independent system commands.

The rightmost button is used to control a pop-up menu containing the currently enabled transformations.

In editors generated for X11, system-command and transformation menus are combined under the control of the right button.

Actuators on the horizontal scroll bar, from left to right, are bound to

page-left
(left-by-half-a-page)
column-left
column-right
(right-by-half-a-page)
page-right

Actuators on the vertical scroll bar, from top to bottom, are bound to

scroll-to-top
previous-page
(back-by-half-a-page)
previous-line
next-line
(forward-by-half-a-page)
next-page
scroll-to-bottom

The mouse is used to move, resize, raise, lower, and iconify windows in the fashion of the given window system and its window manager.

APPENDIX E

Demonstration Editors

A number of demonstration editors and their specifications are included with the release of the Synthesizer Generator. Many are little toys; several are quite substantial; some are quite esoteric. The following list gives a brief description of these demonstration editors.

E.1. Simple Tutorial Editors

dc.syn
    The desk calculator that appears in Appendix A of this manual.

p.syn
    An editor for a simple structured programming language that can serve as an introduction to SSL. Authors: T. Reps, T. Teitelbaum.

chem.syn
    An editor for trivial chemical reactions in which a message (either BAL-ANCED or UNBALANCED) is printed together with an inventory of elements of the left-hand and right-hand sides. Author: T. Teitelbaum

outline.syn
    An editor for hierarchical outlines. Author: T. Reps.

E.2. Editors for Programming Languages

pascal.syn

   A Pascal editor with full static-semantic checking and code generation. Programs can be executed interpretively from within the editor. Authors:
   T. Teitelbaum, K. Mughal, T. Ball, P. Schoaff.

c.syn

   An editor for the C language with full static-semantic checking. The C
   preprocessor is not supported. Authors: S. Liu, M. Belmonte,
   T. Teitelbaum, S. Sinofsky, J. Blandy.

f77.syn

   An editor for FORTRAN 77. Syntax only. Author: S. Sinofsky.

ssl.syn

   An editor for the Synthesizer Generator Specification Language. Syntax
   only. Authors: S. Ahmad, C. Beekhuis, A. Palchoudhuri, S. Sinofsky,
   C. Marceau.

sequel.syn

   An editor for the database query language sequel. Author: S. Horwitz.

E.3. Document Editor

just.syn

   An editor for right-justified, paginated text. Author: T. Reps, A. Zaring.

E.4. Graphics Editor

ideal.syn

   An editor for the Unix graphics typesetting language *ideal* of C.J. Van Wyk.
   Author: B. Vander Zanden.

E.5. Pedagogical Editors

milner.syn

   An editor that does type inference in the style of R. Milner. Author:
   T. Reps.

snelting.syn

   An editor that does type inference in the style of G. Snelting. Authors:
   T. Reps, G. Snelting.

lambda.syn

   A lambda-calculus editor with interpreter. Author: T. Reps.

sethi_ullman.syn

    An editor for arithmetic expressions that compiles and displays optimal code for the expression using the Sethi-Ullman register-allocation algorithm. Author: T. Reps.

toy.syn

    An editor for the language used at Cornell in compiler courses. The editor includes syntax checking, type checking, and code generation for the DEC VAX. Documentation for the language is included. Authors: R. Ashcroft, S. Ghemawat.

ski.syn

    An editor that illustrates compilation into SKI combinators and evaluation by combinator reduction, in the style of D. Turner. Author: T. Reps.

E.6. Logic and Program-Verification Editors

theorem.syn

    A proof-checking editor for sequent-calculus proofs of propositions in integer arithmetic. Authors: T. Reps and B. Alpern.

hoare.syn

    An editor for Hoare-style program logic that embeds the logic from theorem.syn for proving verification conditions. Author: T. Reps.

pv.syn

    An editor for Dijkstra's language of guarded commands, multiple-assignment statements, and integer variables and arrays. Verification conditions are generated and an attempt is made to prove them automatically. Author: W. Pugh.

first_order.syn

    An editor for a constructive propositional logic. Author: T. Griffin.

efs.syn

    An environment for formal systems that allows one to interactively define a logic and prove theorems in that logic. The correctness of proofs is verified incrementally as both proofs and logic are developed. The system supports both Coquand and Huet's Calculus of Constructions [Coquand85] and Harper, Honsell, and Plotkin's Logical Framework [Harper87]. Author: T. Griffin.

APPENDIX F

Syntax of SSL

In the following grammar, nonterminals are printed in Times italic and terminals in Helvetica roman (*e.g. specification* and root). The alternatives of each nonterminal symbol appear indented below it on consecutive lines. The alternatives of *binary-infix-operator* and *unary-prefix-operator* are exceptions and appear on the same line, separated by spaces. The characters $\oplus$, [[,]],]]*, and]]$^+$ have been adopted as meta-symbols. Their meanings are:

$\alpha \oplus \beta$ α or β

[[α]]   optional occurrence of α

[[α]]* zero or more occurrences of α

[[α]]$^+$ one or more occurrences of α

[[α]]$_\beta^*$ [[α [[$\beta\alpha$]]*]]

[[α]]$_\beta^+$ α[[$\beta\alpha$]]*

The following nonterminals denote identifiers:

attribute-name, base-type-name, compile-time-option-name, C-type-name, external-computer-name, parameter-name, function-name, lexeme-name, local-attribute-name, op-name, operator-name, pattern-variable-name, phylum-name, state-name, store-name, style-name, view-name.

specification

    [[*declaration*]]⁺

declaration

    root *phylum* ;

    list [[*phylum*]]⁺, ;

    optional [[*phylum*]]⁺, ;

    optional list [[*phylum*]]⁺, ;

    [[*phylum*]]⁺, { [[*field*]]⁺ } ;

    phylum [[exported]] *function-name*([[*phylum parameter-name*]]*,)
        { *expression* } ;

    phylum ~ [[<*state-name*>]] *phylum.attribute-name* [[*attribution*]] ;

    phylum-name : [[*alternative*]]⁺| ;

    phylum-name ::= [[*alternative*]]⁺| ;

    left [[*token* ⊕*phylum*]]⁺, ;

    right [[*token* ⊕*phylum*]]⁺, ;

    nonassoc [[*token* ⊕*phylum*]]⁺, ;

    transform *phylum* [[*transform-clause*]]⁺, ;

    style [[*style-name*]]⁺, ;

    [[sparse]] view [[*view-name*]]⁺, ;

    phylum foreign *function-name*([[*phylum parameter-name*]]*,
        [[repeated]]) ;

    typedef *C-type-name base-type-name* with (
        op-name, op-name, op-name, op-name, op-name,
        op-name, op-name, op-name, op-name, op-name) ;

    store [[*store-declaration*]]⁺ ;

    ext_computers [[*external-computer-name*]]⁺, ;

    let *compile-time-option-name* = *constant* ;

    forall [[[[list]]*phylum-name*]]⁺, in [[*quantified-declaration*]]⁺ end ;

quantified-declaration
> *phylum* : *operator-name* = *base-type-name* = ;

> *phylum* [[exported]] *function-name*([[*phylum parameter-name*]]$_,^*$)
> { *expression* } ;

> *phylum* foreign *function-name*([[*phylum parameter-name*]]$_,$
> [[repeated]]) ;

alternative
> *lexeme-name* < [[<*state-name*>]] *regular-expression* [[<*state-name*>]]>

> [[exported]] [[*operator-name*]]$_,^*$ [[*parameters*]] [[*attribution* ⊕*unparsing*]]*

> *operator-name* = *base-type-name* =

parameters
> ([[*phylum*]]*)

> ([[*token* ⊕*phylum*]]* [[prec *token* ⊕*phylum*]])

token
> *character-constant*

attribution
> { [[*local-field*⊕*attribute-equation*⊕*view-predicate*]]* }

local-field
> [[readonly]] [[demand]] [[*store-list*]] local *phylum attribute-name* ;

attribute-equation
> *output-attribute* = *expression* ;

view-predicate
> in [[*view-name*]]$_,^+$ on *expression* ;

output-attribute
> *phylum-occurrence.attribute-name*

> *local-attribute-name*

unparsing
> [[[[*view-name*]]$_,^*$ [[@ ⊕ ˆ]] [[: ⊕ ::=]]
> [[*resting-place-denoter*⊕*unparsing-item*]]*]

resting-place-denoter
    @ ⊕ ˆ ⊕ ..

unparsing-item
    string-constant

    phylum-occurrence

    phylum-occurrence.attribute-name

    local-attribute-name

    [[[*unparsing-item*]]*]

field
    [[readonly]] [[demand]] [[*store-list*]] synthesized *phylum attribute-name* ;

    [[readonly]] [[demand]] [[*store-list*]] inherited *phylum attribute-name* ;

transform-clause
    on *string-constant pattern* : *expression*

store-declaration
    store-name phylum with (*op-name* , *op-name* , *op-name* , *op-name*)

store-list
    store ([[*store-name*]]$^{+}_{,}$)

expression
    constant

    variable

    expression binary-infix-operator expression

    unary-prefix-operator expression

    function-name([[*expression*]]$^{*}_{,}$)

    operator-name([[*expression*]]$^{*}_{,}$)

    expression (*expression*)

    [*phylum* |–> *expression* [[, *expression*]]]

    expression [*expression* |–> *expression*]

    expression [*expression*]

    expression [*expression* : *expression*]

$expression$ [$expression$:]

with ($expression$) ([[$pattern$: $expression$]]$_,^+$)

unparse ($expression$ [[, $view\text{-}name$]])

parse ($expression$, $phylum$, $expression$)

$expression$? $expression$: $expression$

let [[[[$pattern$ = $expression$]]$_{and}^+$]]$_;^+$ in ($expression$)

($expression$)

$expression$ { } . $attribute\text{-}name$

$pattern$

    $constant$

    $pattern\text{-}variable\text{-}name$

    *

    default

    $operator\text{-}name$([[$pattern$]]$_,^*$)

    $pattern\text{-}variable\text{-}name$ as $pattern$

$constant$

    [$phylum$]

    < $phylum$ >

    false ⊕ true

    $decimal\text{-}constant$

    $octal\text{-}constant$

    $real\text{-}constant$

    $character\text{-}constant$

    $string\text{-}constant$

    nil

    nil_attr

variable

    phylum-occurrence

    phylum-occurrence.attribute-name

    local-attribute-name

    { [[*phylum .attribute-name* ⊕ *operator-name.local-attribute-name*]]$_,^+$ }

    parameter-name

    pattern-variable-name

    pattern-variable-name.attribute-name

phylum-occurrence

    $$

    phylum

    phylum $ *decimal-constant*

phylum

    phylum-name

    phylum-name [[[*phylum*]]$_,^+$]

binary-infix-operator

    # * / % + − :: @ < <= > >= == != & ^ | && || !

unary-prefix-operator

    − ! ~ & * &&

regular-expression

    character

    string-constant

    character

    [[[*character* ⊕*character* −*character*]]$^+$]

    [^[[*character* ⊕*character* −*character*]]$^+$]

    .

    ^*regular-expression*

    regular-expression$

    regular-expression?

    regular-expression*

    regular-expression+

    regular-expression regular-expression

    regular-expression | *regular-expression*

    (*regular-expression*)

    regular-expression / *regular-expression*

    regular-expression { *decimal-constant* , *decimal-constant* }

decimal-constant
    $[\![1 \oplus 2 \oplus \cdots \oplus 9]\!] [\![\textit{digit}]\!]^{*}$

octal-constant
    $0 [\![\textit{digit}]\!]^{*}$

real-constant
    $[\![\textit{digit}]\!]^{+}.[\![\textit{digit}]\!]^{+}[\![\text{e}[\![+\oplus-]\!] [\![\textit{digit}]\!]^{+}]\!]$

    $[\![\textit{digit}]\!]^{+}\text{e}[\![+\oplus-]\!] [\![\textit{digit}]\!]^{+}$

character-constant
    '*character*'

string-constant
    "$[\![\textit{character}]\!]^{*}$"

character
    $\text{a} \oplus \text{b} \oplus \text{c} \oplus \cdots$

    octal-constant

    $\backslash\text{n} \oplus \backslash\text{r} \oplus \backslash\text{b} \oplus \backslash\text{t}$

digit
    $0 \oplus 1 \oplus \cdots \oplus 9$

Bibliography

Coquand85.
  Coquand, Th. and Huet, G., "Constructions: A higher order proof system for mechanizing mathematics," pp. 151-184 in *Lecture Notes in Computer Science,* Vol. 203, Springer-Verlag, New York, NY (1985).

Demers81.
  Demers, A., Reps, T., and Teitelbaum, T., "Incremental evaluation for attribute grammars with application to syntax-directed editors," pp. 105-116 in *Conference Record of the Eighth ACM Symposium on Principles of Programming Languages,* (Williamsburg, VA, Jan. 26-28, 1981), ACM, New York, NY (1981).

Harper87.
  Harper, R., Honsell, F., and Plotkin, G., "A framework for defining logics," in *Proceedings of the Symposium for Logic in Computer Science* (Ithaca, NY, June 1987), (1987).

Hoover87.
  Hoover, R., "Incremental graph evaluation," Ph.D. dissertation and Tech. Rep. 87-836, Dept. of Computer Science, Cornell University, Ithaca, NY (May 1987).

Johnson78.
  Johnson, S.C., *YACC – Yet another compiler-compiler,* Bell Laboratories, Murray Hill, NJ (July 1978).

Kastens80.
  Kastens, U., "Ordered attribute grammars," *Acta Inf. 13*, 3 (1980), pp. 229-256.

Kernighan78.
  Kernighan, B.W. and Ritchie, D.M., *The C Programming Language,* Prentice-Hall, Englewood Cliffs, NJ (1978).

Knuth68.
  Knuth, D.E., "Semantics of context-free languages," *Math. Syst. Theory 2*, 2 (June

1968), pp. 127-145.

Lesk75.
Lesk, M.E., "Lex – A lexical analyzer generator," Comp. Sci. Tech. Rep. 39, Bell Laboratories, Murray Hill, NJ (October 1975).

Reps82.
Reps, T., "Optimal-time incremental semantic analysis for syntax-directed editors," pp. 169-176 in *Conference Record of the Ninth ACM Symposium on Principles of Programming Languages,* (Albuquerque, NM, January 25-27, 1982), ACM, New York, NY (1982).

Reps83.
Reps, T., Teitelbaum, T., and Demers, A., "Incremental context-dependent analysis for language-based editors," *ACM Trans. Program. Lang. Syst. 5,* 3 (July 1983), pp. 449-477.

Reps84a.
Reps, T., *Generating Language-Based Environments,* The M.I.T. Press, Cambridge, MA (1984).

Reps84.
Reps, T. and Teitelbaum, T., "The Synthesizer Generator," *Proceedings of the ACM SIGSOFT/SIGPLAN Software Engineering Symposium on Practical Software Development Environments,* (Pittsburgh, PA, Apr. 23-25, 1984), *ACM SIGPLAN Notices 19,* 5 (May 1984), pp. 42-48.

Reps88.
Reps, T. and Teitelbaum, T., *The Synthesizer Generator: A System for Constructing Language-Based Editors,* Springer-Verlag, New York, NY (1988).

Stallman81.
Stallman, R.M., "EMACS: The extensible, customizable self-documenting display editor," *Proceedings of the ACM SIGPLAN/SIGOA Symposium on Text Manipulation,* (Portland, OR, June 8-10, 1981), *ACM SIGPLAN Notices 16,* 6 (June 1981), pp. 147-156.

Teitelbaum81.
Teitelbaum, T. and Reps, T., "The Cornell Program Synthesiszer: A syntax-directed programming environment," *Commun. of the ACM 24,* 9 (September 1981), pp. 563-573.

Index

Texts and Monographs in Computer Science

Suad Alagić
Object-Oriented Database Programming

Suad Alagić
Relational Database Technology

Suad Alagić and Michael A. Arbib
The Design of Well-Structured and Correct Programs

S. Thomas Alexander
Adaptive Signal Processing: Theory and Applications

Michael A. Arbib, A.J. Kfoury, and Robert N. Moll
A Basis for Theoretical Computer Science

F.L. Bauer and H. Wössner
Algorithmic Language and Program Development

Kaare Christian
The Guide to Modula-2

Edsger W. Dijkstra
Selected Writings on Computing: A Personal Perspective

Nissim Francez
Fairness

Peter W. Frey, Ed.
Chess Skill in Man and Machine, 2nd Edition

R.T. Gregory and E.V. Krishnamurthy
Methods and Applications of Error-Free Computation

David Gries, Ed.
Programming Methodology: A Collection of Articles by Members of IFIP WG2.3

David Gries
The Science of Programming

Micha Hofri
Probabilistic Analysis of Algorithms

A.J. Kfoury, Robert N. Moll, and Michael A. Arbib
A Programming Approach to Computability

E.V. Krishnamurthy
Error-Free Polynomial Matrix Computations

Texts and Monographs in Computer Science

Now available from GrammaTech, Inc.

The Synthesizer Generator System

The Synthesizer Generator System is available on both a research and a commercial basis. For additional information about how to acquire a copy of the system, write:

> Synthesizer Generator
> GrammaTech, Inc.
> One Hopkins Place
> Ithaca, NY 14850

Also available from Springer-Verlag

The Synthesizer Generator Reference Manual: Third Edition
by Thomas W. Reps and Tim Teitelbaum

The Synthesizer Generator Reference Manual is the defining document of the Synthesizer Generator system. Written by the Synthesizer Generator's creators, this volume provides complete documentation on all aspects of specifying, generating, debugging, and running editors.

ISBN 0-387-96910-1